THE
LONDON
METAL EXCHANGE

a commodity
market

THE
LONDON
METAL EXCHANGE

a commodity market

SECOND EDITION

ROBERT GIBSON-JARVIE
BA (Cantab), FCIArb

Woodhead-Faulkner · Cambridge
Nichols Publishing Company · New York

First published 1976 (in association with Metallgesellschaft AG,
Frankfurt am Main)
Second edition 1983

Published in Great Britain by
Woodhead-Faulkner Limited, 17 Market Street
Cambridge CB2 3PA, England
ISBN 0 85941 221 0

Published in the United States of America by
Nichols Publishing Company, PO Box 96
New York, NY 10024, USA
ISBN 0-89397-173-1

Library of Congress Cataloging in Publication Data
Gibson-Jarvie, Robert.
  The London Metal Exchange.

  Includes index.
  1. London Metal Exchange. 2. Metal trade—Great
Britain. I. Title.
HD9521.9.L6G5   1983   332.64′4   83-13060
ISBN 0-89397-173-1

Typesetting by Hands Fotoset, Leicester
Printed in Great Britain by St Edmundsbury Press,
Bury St Edmunds, Suffolk

Preface

Britain's commodity markets have by tradition been somewhat reticent as to talking about themselves; and this despite the fact that they are of very great importance both directly to those concerned with trading in commodities and indirectly to the economy in general as earners of invisibles and generators of foreign exchange. This contrasts with the situation in the United States, where there is an extensive and for the most part authoritative and readable bibliography available. Some of this is the work of independent authors, but much is the output of the exchanges themselves, which adopt a different stance towards publicising their activities. In recent years the London markets have, it is true, shed some but by no means all of their veil of secrecy, or modesty, and yet they remain in many ways a mysterious area.

As to the London Metal Exchange, when the first edition of this book was being written there was only one other detailed work in existence, and that was by then out of print. This was an excellent study by the Economist Intelligence Unit.

This seemed rather a pity. The LME is in many ways a quite fascinating market, and in its use of the non-transferable principals' contract unique in its field. Apart from what it actually did – and this was important enough to justify more than one in-depth interpretation – what the LME actually was in terms of its human side struck me as something well worth a serious attempt at analysis and description. My aim therefore in embarking on the earlier edition of this book was to interest the reader and if possible instruct him in the development and functioning of a very subtle piece of mechanism, whilst at the same time reminding him that this "mechanism" was in fact made up of people.

In a world of corporate megaliths, the commodity markets are amongst the last surviving bastions of individualism, where disparate and purely subjective opinions and reactions to circumstances are each day drawn together into a real and remarkably accurate consensus. This aspect was brought home to me from the moment I first took up my duties at the LME in Whittington Avenue, after a five-year exile from the City. So also was the strictly empirical approach to new problems – the working-out in the light of past experience in comparable circumstances – which at first I erroneously took to reflect an unwillingness to learn new tricks. If, as one supposes must be the case, pure inventiveness is vouchsafed only to a very few, then an almost infinite adaptability together with a dash of opportunism is the gift essential to a commodity trader.

If it be true that these markets "hold a mirror up to nature" in the economic sense, then it is inevitable that images seen in that mirror will be subject to constant change. It is in their facility for coping with change without undue impetuosity that the strength of the markets lies; and this applies especially to the LME, which is probably the least formally structured of them all. The success or otherwise of a commodity exchange, measured by its capability to carry out its function in the economy as a whole, must rest on the continuing capability of its members to respond and react.

It was this essentially human aspect which led me, in the course of a not very long book, to linger somewhat over the development of the LME over the years in the light of changes in the surrounding climate. My object was to set the Exchange in perspective rather than compile a detailed operational manual.

On returning to the subject after some six years, I found that my general purpose was not altered. There have been developments enough in the interim to justify a thorough bringing of the picture up to date. There have been two entirely new contracts launched, the policy of remaining a principals' market has on more than one occasion had need to be reaffirmed (not least in the debates prior to the setting-up of the Gold Futures Market) and even now the distinction between the LME and other exchanges which this implies is being aired anew. Yet these developments, and the LME's almost beleaguered status in matters pertaining to its basic philosophy, have in a sense strengthened my conviction that, unless the background be clearly shown, the subject matter of the picture is not seen to advantage nor properly understood.

First, then, this book provides an introduction setting out how and why the LME came to be what it is, and only then touches upon matters technical. These latter are, I hope, covered adequately so as to show how the market works without straining the lay reader's patience or expertise – nor, be it said, that of the author.

My qualifications, such as they are, for writing this book were acquired almost by a sort of osmosis. Aside from directly seeking very necessary technical information, one absorbed almost subliminally the essence of a whole wealth of experience through association with those who each individually possessed a part of it. Thus, my teachers were many, and were largely quite unaware of the fact that they were teaching me. However, it would be churlish not to single out in gratitude some particular names: Philip Smith, CBE, and Fred Wolff, CBE, TD (Chairmen respectively of Board and Committee during my years at the LME), Friedrich von Dallwitz and his colleagues at Metallgesellschaft AG, who sponsored the first edition of this book – an act of faith! – and Michael Connor and George Prockter, Committee men both.

June 1983   Robert Gibson-Jarvie

Contents

THE LONDON METAL EXCHANGE

Part Two: The Metals *Page*

Part Two: The Metals *Page*

Part Three: Trading on the LME

PART ONE

An Overview

1

What is a Commodity Market?

Today's commodity exchanges are markets in obligations. A trade carried out across the floor or the Ring is no more, and no less, than the acceptance of a binding obligation by one side to deliver an agreed quantity of the commodity, and by the other side to take delivery of it and pay for it. The date on which this transaction is consummated, the "prompt date", and the price, are agreed at the outset. The market contract lays down that in order to comply with its requirements the commodity offered shall be of an acceptable quality capable of purchase "sight unseen".

By use of this standard contract it has become possible to trade large amounts of most essential raw materials without the need for prior inspection and unnecessary haggle over grade or quality. Pricing on the commodity exchanges is a pure function of supply and demand, not only of the commodity in question but of the money to pay for it, since interest rates, as we shall see later, figure importantly in the making of forward prices.

The open outcry system which is universally employed in trading on the markets, though outwardly chaotic, is probably the optimum possible for arriving with great speed at a price which is competitive (and therefore by implication fair) and where the spread between bid and offer is whittled down to the minimum. But there is a complication: in open outcry trading it is not possible to refuse to trade with any individual who accepts your bid, or who bids to your offer. And you have neither the time nor in all probability the information required to assess how heavily committed he may already be. The *del credere* risk is yours. The world's commodity exchanges have gone their various ways in resolving the credit problem or at least in greatly reducing it. In a later chapter we shall examine the particular method adopted by the LME, but before doing so let us briefly trace the development of the markets to their present-day form and operation.

The long evolution of the exchanges

Whatever its present status in the world of the biologist, the Darwinian theory of the emergence of definable species through the process of adaptation to their surroundings has a definite relevance to the formative process of the world's commodity markets. If all did not start with a common ancestor, then all came into being on account of a trait which is universal in men.

Mankind is at heart a commercial creature. His energies down the ages have been directed more towards trading than towards any other end. Wars are fought for the possession of territory, for development or for defence, as an area in which to live and to trade. Even marriage has its economic side in the consideration of what sort of dowry a bride might bring with her to her husband's estate. (It may be a sad reflection on Western mores that such financial considerations are more applicable today to divorce than to marriage settlements.)

The first international traders were bold men who made journeys, often into unknown territory, in search of goods for barter or for the taking, that they might profitably sell elsewhere. Marco Polo's journey along the Silk Route to China, and Pizarro's storming of South American cities for gold wherewith to enrich his native and warring Spain are but two larger-than-life cases in point.

In later years the apparatus of international trading became more highly developed. There appeared the trading settlements, usually located with good access to the sea, in the areas of production of essential raw materials. Here were gathered in due season the produce of the area for shipment to processing and eventual consumption. On arrival it would be offered for sale in the marketplace and so make for itself its own price, its money equivalent.

This process was made easier by the activities of the Merchant Venturers, whose present-day successors, the merchant bankers and the confirming houses, continue to keep in motion the financial machinery of international trade.

In our own context, though, we shall study the workings of one of

4

the actual markets rather than the banking aspect, save where the latter may be of direct relevance. It may be noted here that this particular aspect may well have been the main reason for the location – to date, at any rate – of the commodity exchanges in the areas of distribution and consumption rather than in the areas of production. The markets, in short, were situated where the money was. This feature is now probably beginning to undergo a process of change as increased wealth and increased sophistication combine with innate commercial acumen to produce a move towards the establishment of commodity exchanges much closer to the producer of the commodity in question.

The first significant step from the straightforward offering of foreign produce in dockside warehouses for sale on the spot was the introduction of the system of trading in "arrivals". Here the deal would be done, and the price agreed, on the basis of a sample available for inspection, for delivery and cash settlement "on arrival of ship". The advantage of arrivals dealings lay in the fact that both seller and buyer now had some form of documentary evidence of a bargain which each, for his own ends, was now in a position to put into the developing banking system for the purpose of obtaining credit.

The system allowed for the break-up of cargoes into smaller parcels, any or all of which might be disposed of in advance of the unloading of the carrying ship. From this stemmed the standard "lot" which is now the unit in any commodity market contract. Thus were established three of the basic characteristics of the exchanges: the fixed contract lot, be it tons, gallons or bags; the price agreed at the outset; and the settlement based on a type-sample of the commodity available for inspection by the intending purchaser.

This last feature has undergone changes, and today the LME operates on a system of approved brands of metal, each of which has been subject to test by a neutral assayer who certifies the acceptability of the brand on the evidence of the sample assayed. The same holds good for deliveries on the London Gold Futures Market.

However, there remained a major disadvantage in dealing simply on an arrivals basis and this was the inevitable uncertainty as to the exact or even approximate time of arrival of a ship. There was also the constant likelihood that wind and weather would combine to make unavoidable the arrival of several ships within a very short period of time. Thus, a condition of alternating surplus and shortage was very difficult to escape.

The actual pinning-down of the date of delivery remained a

matter for crystal-ball gazing until there came fresh developments in the field of technology. The first of these was the steamship, which, though neither so fast nor so sightly as a China clipper with a following wind, did possess the advantage that it could maintain progress on course in a headwind. These steamers were able to forecast their arrival times with reasonable confidence. The second development was that of the undersea cable, by which essential information about ships' departure dates and their arrival in intermediate ports of call could be received in the country to which each was heading well ahead of actual docking.

Now it was possible to set a firm date for the delivery of goods – or at least of their availability for delivery "ex warehouse" or "under tackle" – and the third imponderable was finally nailed down. Today the LME remains unique in trading named days up to three months forward, as distinct from delivery months perhaps further ahead in time. This situation is the outcome of the LME's insistence on seeing itself as a delivery market rather than, or as well as, one with the emphasis on hedging and financially oriented trading. The LME perpetuates the tradition of "spot and forward" rather than pure futures, and in so doing must allow for the possiblity of physical delivery being required at any time. Admittedly, it is problematical whether it would in fact be possible to obtain other than an extrapolated price on the LME for many of the intermediate days between "cash" (spot) and three months forward.

But why this insistence on delivery? Why not simply trade obligations – paper – from the outset? There are several answers to these good questions. In the first place, the answer was very probably the natural desire of the merchant or importer to get his hands on his purchase before parting with his money. And these were all originally merchants' markets: the non-trade element and the speculator had not as yet made their appearance. Another factor was that, had it been possible or even fashionable to buy and sell paper obligations without reference to delivery of the underlying goods, the price of "actuals" – or, in LME parlance, "physicals" – and that of futures in the same commodity would have had no common footing. By at all times presupposing delivery at the end of the day, the two prices – spot and futures – are maintained in relationship one to the other with no temptation to go their separate ways.

Indeed, as was apparent with the passing of the Gaming Acts, any forward contract where there was no provision made for ultimate delivery could have been only a wager on future prices. It cannot be overstressed that the futures price quoted in any commodity market is not a forecast of what the spot price will be on that future date. Rather, it is today's price for a delivery to be effected and paid for on that date, with all that implies as to the storing and the financing of the material meantime.

So, how is it now possible to trade in obligations, that is to buy and to sell all those pieces of paper? This has been made possible by the creation of the clearing house. This is an organisation for clearing – in a sense distributing – futures contracts (not the goods themselves). The clearing house provides a buyer for every seller, and vice versa, and in so doing makes it possible for the seller, for example, of a futures contract to make a later purchase of the same tonnage for the same date and then disappear from the scene, having received or paid only the money difference between the two prices. This apparent magic is achieved by the legal device of novation: the substitution in certain circumstances of one party to a contract by another. With the advent of the cleared contract therefore it became possible to buy and sell futures without loss of the concept of delivery, since the clearing house would merely cause the contractual obligation originally entered into to be passed from hand to hand with payment of any money differences until the prompt date, on which the last open buyer and the last open seller would pay to and deliver to the clearing house respectively.

Though outside our strict terms of reference, since the LME does not make use of a clearing house contract, the principle is important in that it completes the saga of the development of the commodity exchanges. Additionally, it has made possible the introduction of new and exciting markets in other fields such as the purely financial futures exchanges where money itself forms the basis of the underlying security for the contract.

The functions of the markets
Pricing
The very precise and, in several important aspects, complicated mechanism of the market exists essentially to carry out three purposes. The international trade in almost any essential raw material is such that whether it be produced (as with copper) in many parts of the world, or (as with tin) in relatively few, it is very likely that areas of production and consumption will be widely separated both geographically and economically. For this reason the first and perhaps the most important function of a commodity market is to

7

provide a forum at which a fair price may be established on a global basis. Without this, there would be a multiplicity of prices struck bilaterally between individual producers and consumers with little or no common point of reference. The use of the market by representatives of both sides, and from many locations, brings forth a consensus price which all may then make use of in calculating their own prices, taking local or individual circumstances into account.

It should be noted here that one of the several paradoxes of these exchanges is that, in order for this price to be arrived at, only a very tiny fraction of the world's actual consumption of any commodity need be bought and sold on the market. The rapidity of turnover in market contracts ensures that this small proportion is itself traded many times over and this generates the volume of trading necessary for the making of a fair price.

Hedging

The geographical spread of the world's physical trade in commodities, and the fact that they are traded in bulk and thus remain reliant on sea transport, makes it unavoidable that there should be an appreciable lapse of time between leaving the port of departure and unloading in the port of destination. Even where a processor holds an inventory of stocks, he remains in large measure dependent on this comparatively slow-moving *va et vien* of maritime trade. He must therefore place orders for delivery many months ahead, and a great deal may happen during those months which will affect the price he may either have already contracted to pay or be due to pay (whatever it may then be) when he takes delivery of the material.

Both producers and consumers require some protection from the worst effects of a shift in prices adverse to their own interests during the period between inception and fulfilment of a contract to deliver. This protection is gained by hedging in the market, and this is the second function of a commodity exchange. We shall examine hedging, and hedging techniques, on the LME in detail in a later chapter. Suffice it to say here that by trading paper in the market – usually in the opposite sense from physical commitments entered into outside – it is possible so to relate the paper and the physical dealings that a loss on the one will be matched by a profit on the other, thus minimising the element of financial risk endemic in making forward commitments. In an imperfect world the perfect hedge eliminating all such risk is a very rare thing, but the principle of hedging remains valid.

8

Physical dealings

The commodity exchanges have progressed a long way down the road from the time of the mart, where produce was brought and livestock driven for sale for cash or for barter on the spot. Since the earlier days of dealings in arrivals these dealings have tended to become located in or adjacent to banking and financial centres rather than within port areas. The modern market contract provides as a rule for delivery to be effected in an approved warehouse, vault, storage tank or silo in any one of a number of delivery points, usually in the seller's option.

The pricing, hedging and other purely financial market functions, however, now outnumber delivery transactions to an enormous extent, and taking actual material off the market has become practised very much less frequently over recent years. (The LME is something of an exception to this rule, there being appreciably more LME contracts running to actual delivery than in most other markets. But even on the LME it is doubtful whether the figure for deliveries as opposed to contracts closed out exceeds 12.5 to 15%. Something between 3 and less than 1% is typical of most other markets.) For the most part, consumers receive their raw materials for processing direct from producer or merchant under contract. The price will have been settled by reference to the ruling market prices, but delivery is direct and not via the market at all.

At a time of dearth of a commodity consumers look to the market to make up any shortfall in regularly contracted supplies. When a commodity is in surplus, producers tend to sell into the market, not necessarily to consumers but most probably to financial institutions and to speculators. The financier or other non-trade buyer may then use the contracts (taking advantage of the premium of futures prices over spot) as tools in a financing strategy. This we shall consider later, as it is an important side to operating on any futures market, not least on the LME.

So much, then, for the progress of the commodity exchanges from their often quite informal and unorganised beginnings to the highly sophisticated futures markets of today with a whole repertoire of trading techniques which have evolved over the years. What is certain is that however great the degree of this sophistication – and much may be apparent rather than real – it is true to say that the markets have not lost their relationship with the commodities and with those to whom they are quite literally bread and butter. The

9

connection is there, tenuous though it may sometimes appear, and those exchanges which have either lost it or failed in the first place to establish it have themselves faded from the scene.

Now let us turn to a consideration of the LME in this overall context. Where does it fit into the pattern of trading commodities and commodity futures, how does it work, and what makes up the London Metal Exchange?

2
The LME – a Commodity Market

The series of upheavals, events and technological innovations which marked the Industrial Revolution were radically to alter the entire economic and social structure of Great Britain. What had been almost exclusively an agricultural and pastoral economy and one which was largely self-sufficient as to raw materials was rapidly transformed into today's "mixed economy" structure, which necessitates heavy imports of virtually all those raw materials.

Support for this developing import trade, as well as for the brisk entrepôt or third country business which grew along with it, came from the export of finished goods at competitive prices which gave Britain her sobriquet "the workshop of the world". The whole was underpinned by expanding banking and financial services, tending to be concentrated in the City of London.

Metals were no different from the other essential commodities. Domestic sources of supply by now were quite inadequate to meet demand, with the consequence that imports of base metals gained a new significance and an ever-increasing volume.

The beginnings of the LME
Business at first centred on the main ports of entry into Britain, especially those on the western seaboard with access to the Atlantic. As her financial infrastructure developed, however, London was soon competing for business with the Clyde, with Liverpool and with Bristol and Avonmouth. Eventually – and until the outbreak of the Second World War – London was to become the port handling

the largest cargo tonnage. Along with the banks, bill brokers, and insurance and confirming houses, the merchants tended to make London their centre of operations, each specialised trade attracting its members to one or other particular centre within this envelope which was the Square Mile of the City.

For some time the metal merchants in London had been meeting in the Jerusalem Coffee House, off Cornhill, as a necessary adjunct to their regular calls on each other in their own offices. Some sort of central forum was clearly becoming essential, if only at that time for the purpose of exchanging intelligence and opinion.

(The "Jerusalem" deserves a place in history also as the birthplace of the Baltic Exchange, where ship chartering shares a floor with the Grain Market, and whose name was derived from business in grain done with the Hanseatic ports.)

After a period of meeting in the "Jerusalem", as well as of trading along with representatives of many other markets in one of the Walks of the Royal Exchange, the metal merchants decided in 1869 to establish, or at the least to earmark, a rendezvous of their own. By the end of that year the merchants were meeting regularly in the newly opened Lombard Exchange and Newsroom at 40 Lombard Street. (It is a measure of the further specialisation and "local-isation" of areas even within the confines of the City that today Lombard Street would hardly be associated with commodities, which have made their home a few yards further to the eastward in Mark Lane, Mincing Lane and Plantation House.) The Lombard Exchange had been set up as a convenient meeting place for the comparatively large numbers of brokers and merchants in the emerging commodity markets. It thus provided a roof over their heads, a locker or two wherein they might in safety leave their papers and records, and a copying press for their use. However, it was not long before the success of the Lombard in this respect made it less than convenient for the metal merchants. It was overcrowded, it was (they felt) becoming populated too much by a new generation of parvenus jacks-of-all-trades and some of the merchants even reverted to meeting in the Royal Exchange, as a gesture of protest against this development.

However, it was not so much this matter of physical convenience that precipitated the next move, as the then totally unorganised way in which metal prices were established and published. By this time, the market in London was acquiring something of an international reputation, due in the main to the thriving entrepôt business carried on there. It was therefore becoming essential that something positive be done to make it plain to all who were directly or indirectly interested that London prices were fair, representative of the situation day by day, and in no way coloured by any one or a few particular interests.

The Company is established

The establishment of a properly, or rather a formally, constituted body under some kind of centralised control from within, and governed by rules which were applicable to all became a necessity. (Both the Baltic and the Liverpool Cotton Exchange had by now blossomed in this way, and to follow their example would be a logical and constructive move.) To this end, some of the leading concerns co-operated in setting up the London Metal Exchange Company, with its own premises in a room in Lombard Court, in the latter part of 1876. The company held its first meeting on 19 December of that year, and the first meeting of the merchants and brokers under the new aegis was at Lombard Court in January 1877. The capital of the company at the time was £1500.

For a time, progress was both rapid and smooth. Facilities for providing telegraph information were installed, and the first telephone for the use of those present was in operation in 1880: it takes a stretch of the imagination to visualise an LME before that date without the ubiquitous telephone! It is also amusing – from this distance in time – to record that the Exchange's very first Secretary was engaged at about this time at the no doubt respectable salary of £150 per annum.

Subscriptions for membership became obligatory (then, as now, for extremely modest sums) and the beginnings of the "Ring" and "non-Ring" classes of LME membership emerged in the form of London (trading) and Country members.

As yet no attempt had been made to regularise actual trading, or even to limit the number and grades of metals dealt in, although trade in copper and in tin had become predominant. There had been, and for a time was still to be, some business done in pig iron, although this eventually dwindled, while trade in lead and in spelter (zinc) was too heterogeneous as to types and grades to lend itself as yet to any sort of formalisation. Trading times were also crystallised, and official dealings were confined to the periods 12.30 p.m. to 1.15 p.m., and 4.00 p.m. to 4.30 p.m., not so far removed from present-day practice, and at that time without consideration of the London

Silver Market Fixing, or of the time differential between London and New York.

The Ring

Although the lengths of official trading sessions were now limited (with private, member-to-member dealings of course going on continuously around these periods) there was as yet no actual *marché ouvert*. Members continued to transact business in small groups or one with another, disposed in various parts of the Room. The inadequacy of dealing thus, both as to speed and as to the open – and therefore probably fairer – declaration of bid and offer prices was fast becoming apparent.

Those who dealt in copper and tin (the two major metals and those best suited to formal trading in standard lots and grades) very soon created a Ring such as already existed in some of the other commodity markets, where they might all trade freely by open outcry. One of their number would take a piece of chalk from his pocket, draw a large circle on the floor, and all would gather around in what fast became their own established places. The advantages of this system were clear to all; but they could only be fully made use of in a market where transactions were relatively simple and where discussion as to quality, delivery and the like was superfluous. But the basic principle had now been established, and it was to be only a matter of time before dealings in the other metals were so codified as to make Ring trading in all of them a practical possibility. A remarkably efficient and fair, if outwardly chaotic, way of doing a lot of business openly in a very little time had come into being.

After a while friction arose between the body of the subscribers and the Board of the Company, who were felt to be both too autocratic and too divorced from the day-to-day affairs of the market. The main cause for this discontent among the bulk of the members was that the Board numbered only 15 out of a total at the time of over 300 subscribers. Once again, the matter of reporting prices became a source of irritation. The Board had taken this function, along with the issue of a Market Report, to themselves and this was popularly felt to be too narrow a perspective from which to obtain a fair and dispassionate view. A petition was put forward, requesting the formation of a Reporting Committee, which the Board refused.

However (and curiously enough, in retrospect), the final *casus belli* between the Board and the body of the members was – of all

14

things – the decision by the Board in December 1880 to abolish Ring trading. The grounds for what today seems a ludicrously retrograde step were that open outcry dealings led to the manipulation of prices by those with an interest in so doing. In consequence there was no Ring trading throughout the following year, and members perforce reverted to the old practice of strolling from group to group in order to establish prices for what they had to sell or buy. With experience now of very many years of Ring trading with its inbuilt publicity and closeness of bid and offer prices, it is hard to see the logic behind this curious decision to prohibit it. True, there have since then been rare and very brief periods of suspension of Ring dealings – of which more anon.

Their patience running short, the subscribers met in January 1881 and resolved that a Committee of Subscribers be formed, and that its members be elected annually from amongst their number. This was the real beginning of today's structure of the Exchange, and of its unusual hierarchy of Board and Committee: for the directors in 1881 found themselves unable to resist the opinion of the sub-scribers, and the Committee came officially into being after an election in March of that year. Since that time Committee elections have been held in March, with the incoming Committee taking office in April. Happily, the two bodies work today with a large degree of harmony.

The Metal Market & Exchange Company

Today's happy relationship between the Board of the Company and the members of the Exchange was, however, not immediately apparent. The Room was by now felt to be inadequate both to accommodate the large numbers who were in daily attendance, and to maintain the image of the Exchange in the eyes of the world outside it. It is true that a search for more commodious premises had been going on for some time, but until then without result. The commodities trade was by this time becoming established in the area round Mincing Lane, Mark Lane and Leadenhall Street and in consequence the majority of the active trading members of the Metal Exchange had their own offices in this part of the City. The desire for the Market Room to be set up in the vicinity was both logical and strongly felt. At last, one of the members, Mr Kenneth James, formed a group in order to acquire the option on a site in Whittington Avenue, adjacent to the new Leadenhall Market. (This being primarily a meat and poultry market, it is not immediately apparent as to why it should have been felt especially desirable for the Metal Exchange to move into residence there.) However, move it did into a new building, finance for the leasing of which was obtained by setting up a new company – the present Metal Market & Exchange Company – with a capital of £10,000, of which a half was at once taken up. The remaining assets of the old company were absorbed into its successor.

After some delay, the Exchange was installed in its new home in Whittington Avenue in September 1882. It remained in these premises, which were subject to a major refurbishment in 1962 without interruption of trading, until 1978, when the move was made to a new home with better ancillary facilities in Plantation House. The new LME Room is in fact the erstwhile Commodity Exchange.

Subsequent history has happily been one of evolution without undue drama despite the Exchange having to endure and survive two protracted spells of total closure during the two World Wars, when trading raw materials was taken over by the government of the day.

The Company is in fact the proprietor of the Exchange, and its shareholders are the members (subscribers) of the Exchange. Thus, it is hardly a trading company in the accepted sense of the phrase, and at first sight its main function would appear simply to be that of ensuring that the Market premises and their ancillary offices are adequately maintained and staffed, and that funds subscribed by members are put to use in the prescribed way. Sole responsibility for the receipt and payment of money on the Exchange's behalf has in fact always rested with the directors.

The Company's chief sources of income are the subscriptions and Ring fees paid by members, and the proceeds from the sale to members of the standard forms of contracts for use in LME dealings. Both member-to-client contract forms and abbreviated forms for member-to-member trading are issued. Over the years, surpluses have been invested and now there is a further and useful income derived from these investments and from money placed on deposit. For a company standing at the centre of such an important and, in terms of volume of business, such a very large trading body as the LME, the sums actually passing to and from the MM&E Company appear almost ludicrously small, being related only to its function as the proprietor of the Exchange and responsible for meeting its modest logistic requirements.

Apart from acting in a sense as the "upper house" in a bicameral system, the Board bears the sole responsibility for, and is concerned with the financial standing and stability of, members. As a matter of routine, members submit their accounts to the Exchange's own auditors, who in turn refer to the Board any aspect which may merit comment, or where it is felt that elucidation by the member concerned is desirable. The Board is also empowered on its own initiative to seek financial information from any member.

The Committee of Subscribers

There was a time when the members of the Exchange were moved to set up a Committee elected from among their number in order to protect their rights and to assume responsibility for certain duties which they felt were more properly within their province than that of what was, at the time, a somewhat hostile Board. This must have been a hectic moment. Today, the tradition of a Committee of Subscribers dealing with everyday matters and a Board of Directors exercising powers of a more generalised nature is accepted, and it works very well. The Committee acts, to all intents and purposes, as the executive arm of the Market. Its direct responsibilities include such important matters as the standard of dealings in the Ring (and the maintenance of correct discipline and protocol), the daily assessment of prices, the formulation of new contracts, the registration of brands of metal for delivery against an LME contract and the approval of official LME warehouses.

Market discipline, as well as the supervision and the approval for authorisation clerks who work in the Ring on behalf of members, are the major responsibilities of the Standing Committee. This is a smaller body comprising the Chairman and Vice-Chairman of the full Committee *ex officio*, supported by five other senior Committee members. They may also be called upon to act in the rare instances of serious breaches of discipline, or in the sometimes confidential matters arising from investigation of any disagreement between members in the Ring.

The daily assessment of prices (the original reason for the creation of the Committee) is now in the hands of the Quotations Committee, which consists of Committee members assisted by others drawn from a panel of senior subscribers and authorised clerks. One Committee member and two from the panel serve as the Quotations Committee for two-week periods in rotation.

Another, and the most important, function of the Committee is the facility for settling disputes through arbitration. This service is by no means confined to matters arising out of the official LME contracts. It covers disputes emanating from any contract for the purchase and sale of metal where a clause has been included to the effect that disputes arising out of the contract shall be disposed of by way of arbitration under the Regulations of the LME. Thus, a high proportion of the differences which arise from time to time in such an international and highly technical trade are dealt with speedily and without the costs of an action in the courts. Though the Committee meets formally only once each month, in many ways it may be regarded as being in continuous session: groups of its members coalesce, discuss matters and disperse in the course of each day, while a cadre of small sub-committees is maintained for dealing with subjects requiring preparatory work before consideration by a full meeting. This sort of fluidity is essential in a market as lively and as subtle as the LME.

The Executive Secretary to the Committee has the general responsibility for keeping himself abreast and, wherever possible, ahead of developments affecting the Exchange, as well as the more specific duties of assisting and co-ordinating the work of the Committee and its various sub-committees. To this end he works independently of, but in close liaison with, the Secretary to the Company and the other members of the staff.

Board and Committee jointly

There are a number of matters which by tradition, usage or by rule (as enshrined in the Rules and Regulations of the Exchange) have to be dealt with by the Board and the Committee in joint session. Of these, the one of most direct concern here is the election of members with permission to deal in the Ring.

The policy and general conduct of operations on the LME are governed by codified rules, which must themselves have the sanction of the Board before becoming effective. It is here, as well as in the matter of membership, that the Board performs but two of those particular functions mentioned earlier. In this sense, they could be likened with some accuracy to a senate, or upper house by whatever name, in any democratic governmental system. It is popularly supposed (or taken for granted), and to some extent traditionally true, that of the two bodies the Committee are the habitual innovators, with the Board acting as a necessary safeguard in order to ensure as far as possible that innovation is not carried beyond the point of prudence. And the very hazy location of that point in so many cases does indeed make a built-in mechanism for having second thoughts extremely useful. While this generalisation as to the origin of new ideas may on balance have some truth in it, it should not be taken too literally: those with a more detached perspective are often in a better position to see – and to foresee – a problem and to suggest a way over or round it. To this extent they may well have the advantage over those with a direct and daily absorption in Market affairs. In the event, and with remarkably little friction, the two bodies contrive very effectively to oversee the general conduct of the Exchange in its broadest context as well as in detail.

The Committee is elected in March each year with the new Committee assuming office in the following month. Candidates for election must be proposed and seconded by two subscribers, and must themselves be either subscribers or authorised clerks in order to be eligible for nomination. It is undoubtedly a healthy sign of the general interest in these elections that oversubscription by aspirants for election to the Committee is the general rule. In consequence, election by ballot from among the candidates is almost invariably necessary. Subscribers have one vote each, except for the senior subscriber of each Ring member company who receives an additional vote, this in view of the more direct interest in the affairs of the Committee in cases of members who trade in the Ring.

The Board are also elected by the subscribers, who are, as has been noted, the shareholders in the Company. Of the nine members of the Board, three retire each year in rotation and may offer themselves for re-election. In the usual course of events, changes among Board members are infrequent and occur for the most part as the consequence of an individual's own retirement. (There was, however, one recorded instance in the years preceding the last war when a new member was elected to the Board on a wider vote of subscribers after something of a campaign on his part.) Eligibility for election as a director requires the holding of five qualifying shares in the Company. In recent years, a policy seems to have emerged whereby replacements for vacancies on the Board are sought from among a rather wider spectrum than simply from among those intimately connected with the Market. To the extent that this introduces a new element, having perhaps a wider perspective, such a policy would seem to be a happy one. It minimises any risk of direct confrontation between Board and Committee on specific matters of Market procedure – which would naturally be the primary concern of the Committee – or on broader issues, which would come more within the Board's own purview.

In passing, it is worth pointing out that the members of both the Board and the Committee traditionally carry out their duties in these capacities on a voluntary basis. They bear the responsibilities of office in addition to whatever they may be called upon to do as directors, partners or executives in their own organisations. The permanent staff of the LME are not themselves attached to any member, and are the employees of the Company.

The Rules of the LME

It is typical of all commodity markets that their procedures be embodied in a comprehensive, and compendious, set of rules and bye-laws. The LME is no exception. An organisation such as this can function well only if such matters are set out clearly for all to understand, though the rules of the older exchanges, having grown like Topsy over the years and been the work of a succession of more or less skilful draughtsmen, are often somewhat lacking in instant clarity.

Actually, consent to abide by the provisions of the Rules is implicit on payment by a subscriber of his entrance fee and first subscription. It is one of only two ties binding such subscribers together, the other being the obligatory holding of two qualifying shares in the Company.

At first, the only matters set out in the Rules were those pertaining to the qualifications for membership, along with some pretty draconian provisions as to the consequences of a default on a contract. As the contracts themselves assumed a more or less standard form, so their provisions were written into the Rules along with those for the registration of brands of metal eligible for being traded under the contracts, the listing of approved warehouses and the settlement of disputes by arbitration. As the scale of the Exchange's activities increased, along with the element of financial risk which the increase brought in its train, so it became necessary to provide for more rigid financial criteria. Thus, one finds that later inclusions in the LME Rules are predominantly concerned with assuring the health of the market in this respect.

Despite this, one notable feature of the LME Rules (if this is not a contradiction in terms) is the considerable amount of regulatory matter which is in fact omitted from them. On studying the "Blue Book", a reader encountering it for the first time might be excused for marvelling at the almost obsessive attention to detail in such matters as election and voting procedures, and the relative absence of precise trading regulations which characterise the Rules of other exchanges. Trading in the Ring of the LME is in fact a highly disciplined affair, yet very little of what comprises that discipline is laid down in black and white. It is one of the charms – and the source of much of the strength – of the LME that the tradition alone of *fas* and *nefas*, or what is "done" and "not done", should be held in such respect.

The unique double-headed constitution of the LME with its Board of the Company and Committee of Subscribers necessitates a number of somewhat recondite provisions concerning the "balance of power" between the two bodies. Of the two, the Committee is generally more concerned with matters pertaining directly to trading, with the result that most of the Rules relating to contracts, brands, market discipline (in so far as it is actually spelt out) are the fruits of the Committee's labours. Those concerning the financial integrity of the Exchange and, as far as may be legislated, of its members emanate for the most part from the Board. But no matter who may be the author or instigator of any new Rule, or alteration to an existing one, it is the Board which must must sanction it.

Surprisingly enough, the system of control of the market being shared between Board and Committee has worked very well over the years since that historic moment when the first Committee of Subscribers was formed. The Rules themselves provide for what should be done in the event of deadlock over any matter of importance – there should be a meeting of subscribers – but there seems no hard evidence of one ever having been necessary for this purpose, although meetings are not unheard of for the discussion of other matters.

In truth, this happy history must be the outcome in large measure of the personalities and common cause of those elected to the two bodies over the years.

3

The Philosophy of the LME

Under this resounding heading we shall examine further the structure and rationale of the Exchange in the light of the responsibilities borne by its various components. This should in turn lead us towards an understanding of LME procedures and practices. The most important among these are the ones which single this market out as being outstandingly different from all its contemporaries.

Perhaps the trait which most distinguishes the LME from other commodity markets is the importance attached there to the individual and to individuality in market dealings. Even the LME contract is a purely bilateral affair between buyer and seller. Its obligations are not transferable by novation as they are on cleared markets and there is no central guarantee body: each party looks to the other only.

LME membership
Membership has always been a purely personal affair. Members, once elected and subject to annual re-election, are individuals and not corporations, although today the majority are representatives of the corporations which they serve. The status of Individual Subscriber as distinct from that of Representative Subscriber remains, but the number of those enjoying it grows smaller. More recently a third category, that of Honorary Member, has been established: they have no say in the management of the Exchange,

save perhaps by influence, nor the opportunity to trade in the Ring.
But they pay no subscription, either.

In its early days the LME consisted only of an informal gathering
of merchants whose common ground was that they occupied themselves with physical trading in base metals. It would not be a gross
inaccuracy to say today that a very respectable proportion of current
members – though by no means all of them are merchants as such –
share this common overriding interest. The commission houses
acting for a different clientèle are in a minority on the LME at least
in terms of Ring membership.

In order to do business in the Ring of the LME, a company must
first be represented by a Representative Subscriber. Within limits,
his status in his own company is not strictly material in the eyes of
the Exchange. He will be looked to as the personification in the
LME of the body which he represents, and to do this to the LME's
satisfaction he need not inevitably be Chairman or Chief Executive.
Once a Representative Subscriber has been admitted, his company
is at liberty to nominate one or (more frequently) several Clerks.
These may be Ordinary or Authorised Clerks. The latter are more
experienced, and, having undergone a period of probation and
passed an oral examination conducted by the Committee, they are
authorised to trade in the Ring on their company's behalf. (The
status of Authorised Clerk was instituted in 1883, which indicates
that even at that early date in the history of the Exchange the
principal trading on his own account – the prototype LME member
– was being joined on the market by employees of fellow members.)
This remains the most common arrangement: once the Representative Subscriber has been granted "Ring dealing privileges" (note
that he is not granted "rights"), he generally deputes the actual
attendance in the Ring to his Authorised Clerks while maintaining
his own Subscriber status within the Exchange, and concomitant
rights to attend and vote at Subscribers' meetings.

While there are a number of organisations – for the most part
those either acting as brokers for outside clients or concerned with
the metals trade but without need for any degree of direct LME
activity – who are content with Ordinary Member status for their
Representative Subscribers, there are a substantial number whose
business makes it at the least desirable if not totally vital to have
Ring dealing privileges. These latter are the companies actively
engaged in hedging and pricing their own, their associates' or their
clients' intake or output, as well as the larger commission houses

trading their clients' positions, to all of whom the extra subscription for Ring membership, with its other commitments, is worth paying.

There is, indeed, a purpose in, and benefit to be derived from, what the LME calls "non-Ring" membership. Apart from being as it were one of the family (although owing to space limitations no longer able to enter the trading room in which the Ring is situated) the Subscriber for a non-Ring company has his say in the running of the Exchange and a vote at any formal proceedings. As will be outlined in a later chapter, non-Ring companies also share the VAT concessions applying to trading on a terminal market.

The criteria for Subscribership on behalf of a Ring member organisation are not surprisingly set at a higher level than those applicable to non-Ring companies. In both cases a respectable track-record in metals trading is essential, but the Ring member must also demonstrate his ability to stand behind all his dealings on the market in the financial sense. There being no overall guarantee of Ring members' open positions, each must carry the financial responsibility for them in addition to the *del credere* of his own clients.

The demands on an applicant for Ring dealing privileges may be subject to variation from time to time. Currently they include the demonstration of a "margin of solvency" of not less than £500,000 and provision of an independent bank guarantee for a like amount. Where the applicant is a member of a group, a guarantee by the parent company is also required, in a sum as laid down by the Board and Committee in joint session. There are certain other requirements and these will be considered when we study the collective security of the Exchange.

There are no restrictions as to the proprietorship of any company represented by a Subscriber: indeed there could be none. Thus, companies with foreign parentage or affiliations are free – on meeting the criteria – to be represented; of the Ring members at least one half are owned or controlled from outside the United Kingdom. There remains, however, the requirement that all organisations directly represented in the Ring be incorporated in the United Kingdom (whatever their parents' location) and have a preponderance of UK-domiciled directors or partners.

As a result – at least in part – of these somewhat onerous conditions for Ring membership, the pattern has emerged in recent years of the majority of Ring members being the specialised "arms" of much larger and frequently multinational organisations. The independent firm trading in the Ring on its own account has become very much the exception rather than the rule. The LME has come a very long way from being the informal gathering point for like-minded merchant proprietors with a direct interest in trading physical metal. Such a progression was to some extent at least to have been expected: for better or worse businesses do expand and they do merge. But it may also be argued that by its very obduracy in holding to the concept of the principals' contract, the Exchange has, as a result of its unavoidable financial demands in the pursuance of this policy, made the lot of the smaller independent no longer economically supportable. In many ways this is not an unmitigatedly happy outcome, for a leavening of independents can be an effective brake against any tendency to excessive polarisation between fewer though larger interests.

The security of the Exchange

The security of the Exchange has increasingly come to the forefront in the minds of its Board and Committee. Time was, when the proprietors dealt on their own account, that the financial demise of one of them was a matter for regret at another's misfortune but not of itself cause for any qualms amongst his fellows as to their own position. Each dealt, and was in a position to deal, within prudent limits.

Since those very early days two developments have changed the picture pretty comprehensively. In the first place, business was generally expanding to no mean degree in the prosperous years leading up to the outbreak of the First World War. And if after the post-war resumption of trading there was a period of quietude during the years of the Great Depression, this was followed by the emergence of a trend (which accelerated almost day by day in the decades following the Second World War) towards the carrying out in the market of orders on behalf of clients quite unconnected with the LME. Not only were the Ring members doing more business for their own, frequently affiliated, trade clients in the hedging and pricing area, but they were also increasingly trading for a new species of non-trade client. Thus they found themselves carrying the risk of heavy clients' positions which they traded off to the best of their ability amongst each other in LME Ring dealings.

One very important aspect of an open outcry market such as the LME is the fact that it is not possible for a participant to decline to trade with any other. Once a price has been called – be it bid or offer

25

– the whole purpose of the market is to ensure that a positive response constitutes a trade and therefore the commencement of a contractual obligation. And, when made, these responses must be treated on a "first come, first served" basis. Additionally, it is extremely difficult for any member of the market to have more than the most approximate idea of the financial exposure of any of his fellows. One who has been seen to be selling or buying heavily may be "back to back" with a secure commitment in physicals, or he may be operating for a client with impeccable credentials. There is no way of knowing; and on the LME once a member has traded with another he remains locked into a contractual situation with him until the prompt date. Conversely, in a clearing house market a member is automatically relieved of this responsibility on registration of his trade and payment by both sides of the initial margin. Whilst each must bear the *del credere* in so far as his outside clients are concerned, the clearing house assumes the risk member to member.

The difference between the two kinds of market has not of course been lost on the LME, several of whose members are additionally members of one or other cleared exchange. There has been, and will no doubt continue to be, a good deal of lively debate on the subject. There have also been some rather more specific attempts made at arriving at a compromise between the fully cleared market and the "principals only" ethos of the LME derived over its years of trading. A study was carried out by the (then) London Produce Clearing House in 1968 for a cleared market in silver, and in 1973/4 another for a modified form of the American style of mutual clearing corporation was carried out by the author.

But it remains a matter of balancing the arguments for and against. In the eyes of the LME the advantages of the present system outweigh those of a cleared one. And it has to be pointed out that at no time in its long history has the LME been in any way embarrassed by the failure of one of its members. Failures there have been – how else in the world of international commerce? – but they have been quite adequately dealt with and nobody outside the Exchange has suffered in consequence.

However, the LME method still remains something of an enigma to those outside it (and to some within) who are habituated to the methods of a cleared market. The extensive off-market or "inter-dealer" trading between members of the LME is a case in point. To some, this represents a facility for trading almost literally round the clock, as well as a very efficient way of matching orders without the need to trade them in the Ring. To others, the very thought of unregulated and unrecorded off-market dealings is something of an anathema. (On purely practical grounds it has to be admitted that interdealer trading does make impossible, for example, the keeping of accurate records as to turnover and even as to the daily run of prices.)

After earlier rejection of any modification of trading practice which would impair the inviolability of the non-transferable contract, there remained the strong and no doubt correct current of opinion to the effect that something be done which afforded at least some protection from the potentially disastrous consequences of a major default spilling over to others than the defaulter by the "domino effect". One new provision made in 1975 was that in addition to their normal contributions to the LME Compensation Fund each Ring member should covenant with the trustees of the Fund to contribute up to a maximum of £100,000. This sum, or a part of it, was to be called only if, in the opinion of the Board and Committee, the sum required to compensate one or more Ring members from loss due to the default of any other Ring member was such that to meet the whole amount from the Compensation Fund or from "any other available source" (which is not specified) would cripple the Fund. Contributions from the £100,000 covenanted by each Ring member are to be made on a *pari passu* basis with each paying a like amount.

To date this provision has never, happily, had to be put into practice. But its existence – enshrined in the complicated and rather prolix Rule 16 of the LME – serves to exemplify the lengths to which the LME is prepared to go in order to safeguard and perpetuate its traditional method of direct principal-to-principal trading.

Shortly afterwards there was devised what does seem to show all the signs of an acceptable compromise between principals trading and clearing, though the mechanism contains no actual element of clearing in the strict sense. Without going deeply into the workings of "MEMO" (Metal Exchange Monitoring Operation), a system was evolved whereby the market exposure of Ring members is monitored on the basis of returns submitted daily by each to an external computer bureau – actually, the International Commodities Clearing House. The returns are then scrutinised by the "Monitor" – a firm of accountants – who are in a position to deduce each Ring member's open indebtedness in the light of current prices, compare

27

this with his permitted open indebtedness, and report any excess to the LME's Monitoring Committee. The system works on a "no names, no packdrill" basis until the point is reached at which the Monitoring Committee are advised by the Monitor of an excessive position. The Committee can match the member's numbered code with his name and are empowered to call him to order in whatever way they see fit. Here again, we see the LME keeping its internal discipline very much to itself.

The "pre-Market" and interdealer trading
One further matter merits our attention in considering the philosophy of the LME: its approach to the business of establishing what one might call a datum or benchmark upon which the day's pricing activity is to be founded.

Buyers and sellers alike need to have a close idea of what prices are likely to be attractive and to lead to a trade being done which is acceptable to both. It is important that neither should waste valuable time with preliminary bids and offers which are separated by an unnecessarily wide gap. Apart from this time-wasting aspect, in highly competitive trading the party without an adequate perception of opening prices in advance runs a real risk of being left hopelessly behind while his competitors, being closer to each other's offers and bids, are striking the bargains.

In short, there has to be provision for some means of testing the market, for obtaining quotations, or "indications" in commodity market parlance, without necessarily making a commitment. From these informal and usually bilateral "probings" may be formed a good approximation of prices to be expected when Ring trading commences.

Certain other markets habitually do all their buying and selling in this way: witness the Baltic and The Stock Exchange. Others bring offers and bids gradually into balance at a single going price by amassing the largest number possible received from outside, whilst members of the market are assembled together. This is the method adopted by the London Gold Fixing and by the cash (physical) tin metal and tin concentrates market in Penang. It could possibly have been the foundation for much more accoustically genteel commodity exchanges had they followed that particular line.

What happens in an open outcry market can take two forms. In the "soft" commodity markets and the London Gold Futures Market there is a formal call to market at certain times during the day, and invariably on the opening and before the closing of trading for the day. A Call Chairman conducts this exercise, during the course of which bids and offers are made for each delivery month in turn and a firm buyer's and seller's price arrived at for each. Thus, the supply and demand factor is identified until the next call; in between calls random outcry trading continues without a break.

In these markets interdealer trading, or trading off the floor, is not permitted. They hold that all dealings must be conducted on the floor and, in the market context, in public. This is not so on the LME, where pre-Market trading member to member by telephone or by VDU from their own offices performs this price-determination function. Such trading, conducted by the members individually, is not recorded in any official statistics, a fact which can confuse those who are not LME members and who are more attuned to the call system in London and to the systems in use in the United States.

The principals' contract on the LME makes it quite practical during interdealer trading for members actually to do deals, in addition to exchanging indications as to prices at which they might be willing to buy or to sell. There is no registration of contracts with a central clearing house and, in theory at least, no need and certainly no compulsion to bring all dealings to the Market floor. Thus, any LME member may match clients' buying and selling orders where they are in line as to price and prompt date by dealing with each direct and leaving himself with a net long or short position (or a net price difference) either to carry in his books or to trade off with fellow members in the Ring.

As we shall see when we consider pricing on the LME, this facility for dealing before the commencement of Ring trading is an important factor in "back-pricing" by consumers.

There is of course no obligation on a client to have his orders dealt with in this way. On placing any order with his LME broker he has only to state the requirement that it be carried out in the Ring for this to be assured.

However, the LME's approach to the matter of setting prices in perspective before outcry trading commences is not universally popular amongst those used to the call market tradition. It, and its real purpose, are frequently called into question, largely through an imperfect understanding of that purpose. It does at first sight seem to be something of a contradiction in terms for an open outcry market to permit bilateral trading off the market with its unavoidable impairment of true "price transparency". It would not be feasible

29

for the LME to convert to a call system without first abandoning its facility for trading named dates rather than delivery months. On weighing the pros and cons of both approaches (and these were brought into sharper focus during early discussions when the gold futures market was first proposed), the LME remains in favour of its traditional way as that best suited to the demands made on it by those who daily bring their business there.

In this chapter we have perhaps indulged ourselves in our consideration *in extenso* of various aspects of the LME's make-up. Each of them has a relevance, however, and paying attention to them may assist the obtaining of a better grasp of what motivates the LME as an entity. It is hoped that this will serve a useful purpose in setting into their proper perspective the less generalised chapters which follow and thus adduce a fuller appreciation of this unique exchange and its way of going about its business.

4
LME Contracts

Dealings in arrivals laid the foundation for standardising many of the more important terms in forward-dealing contracts. The size of the contract lot, the agreed quality (per sample) and the method of settlement were already capable of being set down in a standard form of wording. Missing, in those days, were the fixing of a settlement or "prompt" date – be it a named day as on the LME or a delivery month – and the naming of a formalised body under whose authority and according to whose rules the contract was written.

The LME is a multi-commodity exchange where several metals are traded. Each has its own peculiarities, and yet each contract contains a number of conditions which are common to all.

The first official LME contracts made their appearance in 1883. They applied only to dealings in copper and tin, which at the time were the only metals traded in sufficient volume for an attempt to specify terms of trading to be worth while or even practicable. Originally there were four distinct standard contracts: for the sale of metal in warehouse to be effective on a fixed date; again for metal in warehouse but with an open or undefined prompt date; for metal "now landing"; and for metal for sale "on arrival". The first of these was to survive and become the basis of the current LME standard contract: sale of metal in warehouse for delivery and settlement on a named date.

The conditions which are common to all LME contracts are as follows.

Forward periods

The forward period permissible was early set at three months, this being the average voyage time for copper *en route* from Chile via Cape Horn, and for tin from the Malay Straits via the Cape of Good Hope. With the exception of a seven-month period for silver – now abandoned for lack of use – these have remained the forward periods to this day.

From the outset, the prompts in LME contracts have been for trading days rather than delivery months: a characteristic which remains peculiar to the LME. It is possible that the universal use of the delivery month on the "soft" commodity markets has its origin in the seasonal nature of the produce traded and its comparatively brief storage life, which would presuppose its sale for processing and consumption very soon after its unloading. The in-warehouse delivery on the LME of material which can remain unspoiled in store almost indefinitely makes it more simple to fix a day for its uplift almost regardless of its date of entry into the warehouse. It is also an important fact that the tendering and delivery procedures adopted in a clearing house market make daily prompts difficult if not impossible to arrange – a point to be taken into consideration were the LME ever to consider adopting a clearing house system.

A forward period longer than three months would almost certainly entail if not a full clearing then at least a far more rigid enforcement of variation margins since financial exposure in a moving market increases in step with the length of time a contract remains open and uncovered. Some options, and certain dealings in physicals, may be, and frequently are, traded for considerably longer periods than three months; but these are not official LME dealings and may not be carried out in the Ring.

The standard lot

The warehouse warrant is the LME's "unit of currency", and warrants are issued by approved warehouses which cover set tonnages of metal. Though they do vary between one metal and another, the concept of trading in multiples of the standard warrant lot is common to all LME contracts.

For practical purposes a weight tolerance is provided for in the contract, as well as a defined measure of latitude as to the shape and weight of individual pieces making up a warrant. In LME accounting, trades are settled at the price agreed on the basis of the exact tonnage specified in the contract: 25 tonnes of copper, 6 of nickel, 5 of tin and so forth. When the warrants change hands, any marginal discrepancy between the "round tonnage" and that actually shown on the warrant is accounted for between buyer and seller on the settlement price of the previous day.

Delivery point at seller's option

The LME maintains a list of approved warehouses, and vaults for silver, in listed delivery points. Though not particularly large, the number of these points is such that, were the choice to rest with the buyer who wished to take physical delivery, it would follow that sellers must either maintain a stock of warrants for each delivery point or be faced with arranging a warrant "swap" each time a buyer named a point at which the seller held no warrants. This means that the buyer may himself be faced with a swapping problem should he need delivery in a point other than the one where the warehouse whose warrant he has received is situated. As is the case in all markets where futures are traded, only a small proportion of LME contracts run to delivery as most buyers of physical metal do so under contract direct with their suppliers, but with prices based upon those made in other dealings on the LME. Trading on the market itself is primarily for the purposes of hedging and pricing, and such dealings are for the most part closed out on the prompt date with no actual delivery. Location of the metal in such cases is of no account.

The matter does, however, have much significance for the LME Committee when consideration is being given to the authorisation of new delivery points. There are those who in principle favour a wider network of such points – spread over a large geographical area – to encourage more producers to offer their material as an LME-registered brand for trading in the market. Thus, it is argued, is the market improved and made more comprehensive as a hedging and pricing forum by the accumulation of more "chips" for trading. The converse argument holds that to increase the number, and in particular the spread, of delivery points too much will lead to further complications for those wishing to take actual delivery in a location of the seller's choosing. This, it is held, could actually discourage a measurable segment of the trade from using the LME.

Producers, too, are often said to be chary of seeing material bearing their name distributed through the workings of the market in directions and to destinations over which they have no control.

33

One possibility which is canvassed from time to time in the light of the worldwide distribution of industrial metals is the establishment of a formalised exchange of warehouse warrants, with premiums or discounts publicly announced. This would, its proponents argue, be an improvement over bilateral negotiation in a warrant swap, and pave the way for a much wider spread of delivery points whilst preserving the principle of the seller's option as to location.

Provision for dealing with disputes

As with the majority of commodity markets, the LME stipulates in its contracts that any dispute arising out of the formation or the performance of any contract be referred in the first instance to arbitration. The arbitration rules are actually set out in full on the reverse of the contract issued to clients. Before any litigation may be instituted, the full arbitral procedure must be gone through.

The principals' contract

This is the feature which distinguishes the LME contracts from those issued under the rules of any other terminal market.

We have already noted in a previous chapter the LME's attitude towards, and procedures in connection with, the financial integrity of the Exchange and of its members. At this point we should simply take note of how the contracts themselves stand in defining the mutual relationship of the parties.

The LME does not make use of a clearing house (the "clearing" of Ring members' contracts is quite a different thing), and in consequence there is no novation process whereby one party to a contract may be substituted for another. Hence the phrase in the standard form: "This contract is made between ourselves and yourselves as principals, we alone being liable to you for its performance." The clause goes on to state that whatever percentage is charged by the member to the client is to be regarded as a part of the price; note that it is not a separate commission as applies on other markets. This point was to stand the LME in good stead in the adaptation of value added tax to its dealings.

The bilateral nature of the LME contract makes the calling of initial and variation margins a matter for the discretion of the issuing member. Thus, whilst there is a standard paragraph which sets out the rights of the member to call margin "up to an amount not exceeding the value of the contract" – a pretty draconian measure were the member to exercise the right – the actual calling, and the actual amount of any margin, is individual and not laid down save in the contract for silver. This is an instance of a standard clause providing for an unstandardised procedure, which is made necessary by the bilateral nature of the contract. It is, however, important to note than on the LME any margin requirement is specifically to be set by the members as individuals on a contract-by-contract basis, and not by the Exchange itself, or by a clearing house, on an overall one.

Before leaving the terms which are common to all the contracts by inclusion, one notable exclusion commands our attention. It should be noted that the LME contract contains no mention of any form of *force majeure*. Delivery of the warrants by the seller – be he the member or the client – is implicit. The only concession is that contained in Rule L of the contract rules (set out on the reverse of the client's form of contract), which provides that a seller may with the prior approval of the Committee delay actual delivery if such is for any reason physically impossible – but only if he can satisfy the Committee that he was the possessor of the metal required in an approved delivery point at least 10 days before the contract became prompt, or that he has it on his own premises. This is a very limited concession, referring as it does only to outside influences which prevent for a short time the discharge or the warehousing of metal for placing on warrant. In no other circumstances may inability to deliver a warrant backed by metal be cited.

So much, then, for the provisions which are common to all LME contracts. Members' individually printed forms (where they are used) must be expressed to be subject to all the standard terms as though they were actually printed on them. The provisions which differ the one from the other are those which refer to contractual peculiarities in trading the various metals and are concerned with technicalities as to weights and specification.

PART TWO
The Metals

5
Copper

One of the two original LME standard contracts, that for Chile bar copper, was also the first to be modified in the light of experience of physical trading. This arose as a consequence of the decline in Chilean production, which at first had accounted for most of the UK trade in that metal, to the point where in the 1880s it comprised a mere 12.5% of LME business in copper. The USA had by this time emerged as the biggest supplier. In 1882 output from the Anaconda mine began to be offered on the export market, and by 1885 American output had all but doubled: to a total of 74,000 tons. World output that year was over a quarter of a million tons (an increase of 25% in the period since 1882), with Spain and Portugal also producers of considerable quantities.

The market was not at the time capable of absorbing such a tonnage, and the LME price (for Chile bars) fell from £66 10s 0d in 1882 to £38 7s 6d in 1887. Such an appreciable and prolonged fall in price naturally had the effect of encouraging consumers to run their own stocks down, and to purchase on a hand-to-mouth basis rather than hold in their inventories metal which was steadily declining in value. Despite these developments, it was still quite feasible for physical transactions in Anaconda and other brands to be priced and hedged on the LME against the Chile bar contract, since prices taken overall were still keeping fairly evenly in step. However, it was appreciated on the LME itself that the Chile bar contract was no longer representative, and was already well on the way to becoming solely a hedging or "paper" one. This was not a development which those in authority wished to encourage, with the needs and the traditions of a delivery market uppermost in their thoughts.

Apart from the "paper" or speculative aspect now presented by the Chile bar contract, dealings in this metal had declined to a point where it was not in a position to supply sufficient market chips even to perform the hedging function adequately. With hindsight – viewing from this point in time – the market was ripe for a squeeze.

The Secretan Syndicate

This in fact is precisely what ensued. Pierre Secretan, Manager of the French firm Le Société des Metaux, conceived the idea of cornering the by now limited supplies of copper on the market, and so holding it to ransom until such time as it was prepared to pay his price. (This was the earliest recorded squeeze on the LME, and in terms of the economics of its time possibly the largest. Now it has been followed by others, and the temptation to try to corner a market will probably always be present in some minds in some circumstances. It is a function of any free market to frustrate or at worst strictly limit the ill effects of any such exercise.)

Secretan also operated in tin, but the bulk of his dealings were in copper and the "Secretan Corner" is generally regarded as forming a part of the history of that market. He – or his syndicate – started buying in the autumn of 1887, and prices at once commenced rising. His own purchases were followed by those of anxious consumers, whose own low inventory stocks now began to appear inadequate if replenishment were to be at a sharply increasing cost to themselves against a rising market. By the end of 1887 Chile bars had risen from £39 10s 0d to £85. Shares in mining houses had also advanced (and Secretan was speculating in this field, too), to the extent that before long the Bourses were flooded with issues of shares at high premiums in new and dubious mining companies.

It was not long, however, before the inevitable consequences of a squeeze operation began to be felt. Producers who had until then seen the price of their material declining in an over-supplied market, and who had in consequence begun holding back deliveries, now found that the market was rising steeply – riding on the back of the inflated price of Chile bars. They recommenced offering copper on to the market in order to release their own high stocks and take advantage of the trend in so doing. At the same time (and this is particularly relevant in the case of copper) large quantities of scrap began to come forward. The copper market always has this big

40

element of secondary material refined from scrap; and this is regarded as one of the main obstacles to any sort of real control of the copper market by the primary producers.

Secretan was compelled to buy increasing quantities in order to maintain his grip on the market. His financial needs grew at an even greater rate, since prices were now rising fast – at his own instigation. Furthermore, in order to be successful he needed to keep these prices up: when the market finally surrendered and came to him as the only seller, he had to realise figures which would both repay his financiers and show him his speculative profit. (Secretan's main financial backers at the time were the Comptoir d'Escompte and Rothschilds in Paris, and Baring Brothers in London.) By the spring of 1888 the syndicate could lay hands on capital to the surprising sum of £2.5 million, and Secretan was emboldened by this to the extent of negotiating with the major overseas producers to buy their output over the next three years at or in excess of guaranteed prices to them. These producers for their part undertook to restrict output to current levels, and Secretan, secure on this front, continued to absorb the greater proportion of any copper from other sources which found its way on to the market in London.

It was a situation which by its nature could not last. Eventually, market forces inevitably prove stronger – or more enduring – than even the best-backed manipulator. The Secretan Syndicate first relinquished its grip on the tin market, and the copper "corner" finally collapsed in the spring of 1889. By the time this happened, stocks of copper in Europe had all but trebled during 1888 and the first months of 1889, and the syndicate was borrowing sums approaching £6 millions in order to finance its by now impossibly burdensome holdings (at an average LME price of £76 per ton, the Secretan holdings must have been in the region of 75,000 tons). Purchases for cash – immediate delivery – by the syndicate ceased after February 1889; and following the suicide in March that year of the Secretary of the Comptoir d'Escompte, the bank itself was saved from disaster by a support operation mounted by the Banque de France. Meanwhile, the London price of copper collapsed from £75 to £35 per ton within the first half of March, having previously touched a record £105, with attendant wide backwardation.

The syndicate's stocks had been taken over by the Banque de France and their liquidation posed a major problem: too fast and the market would be unable to absorb them without a further decline in prices, and too leisurely a programme would leave the bank virtually maintaining Secretan's erstwhile monopoly position. In fact the process took several years and in 1890 its progress had stabilised average prices at around £54 5s 0d per ton.

It is interesting to speculate on how this affair might have worked itself out had the Secretan Syndicate operated in the three months position, rather than in cash copper, lending the warrants in the market as contracts became prompt.

Further attempts at control – the Amalgamated Copper Company

After the Secretan operation, the first serious attempt by a producing group to control prices was made in the 1890s. The approach had now been made "from the other end" so to speak, and was based on agreed curtailment of production by mining groups. However, co-operation by all such groups (notably the Americans, who at the time were responsible for some 50% of world output) was no easier to ensure then than has proved the case in more recent times.

In 1899 certain significant changes in the proprietorship of Anaconda, followed by the absorption of other Montana mines, resulted in the creation of the Amalgamated Copper Company. This group was of itself large enough to obtain the co-operation (willing or not, history does not relate) of other American producers as well as of the Spanish. Shipments of Amalgamated production to Europe were reduced, and in consequence the price of standard copper in London rose from an average of £51 (or just over) to more than £73 per ton. For a time, the producers were able to buy on the market as an aid to maintaining prices at these levels, but continuing demand by consumers even at these prices led to increases in output by producers outside the group. As a result, the support operation became unduly costly, and inevitably large stocks of metal were piling up in Amalgamated's hands.

The pendulum swung abruptly (as later experience shows will always be the case when a corner or a cartel finally collapses) and heavy selling in both London and New York brought standard back to £45 per ton by early 1902. Once again, heavy stocks – this time in producers' hands – had to be liquidated without further upsetting the market, and once again the LME rose to the occasion. For a time in the first decade of this century, American speculation in mining shares as well as further attempts by Amalgamated to hold back supplies of copper resulted in much instability of prices: at one time (in 1907) standard was priced at £112 in London. Later, the collapse of business confidence in the United States brought all prices down once more, and the market lapsed into a calmer though somewhat depressed state.

Copper – and cartels – between the World Wars

At the end of the First World War, the United States was established as the dominant producer of copper, in line with her generally fortunate economic situation in the early post-war years. For the most part, America's domestic production was absorbed by her own fabricators and she was not (nor has since been) a major exporter. However, at that time America largely controlled the Chilean and other Latin American mines and, though their output tended in the main to go to the United States for smelting, it was then widely exported, accounting for some 66% of world exports. The emerging Congolese production was also to a large extent refined in the United States. Of the other "independent" producers, Spain was no longer a serious factor and the other African mines were not yet consolidated to anything approaching their present importance as exporters. Unfortunately for them, the American interests now found amongst their overall holdings numerous mining operations which for various reasons were less profitable than the others – the so-called "high cost" mines. Expansion of production from other sources militated against higher prices and once more the attempt was made to control output in order to support or increase world copper prices.

Copper Exporters Incorporated was formed in 1926. Apart from American and Chilean producers its members included Rio Tinto, Katanga (Congo) as well as German interests, and in all they accounted for no less than 95% of world production. This cartel professed the aim of supporting copper prices by the exclusion of speculators and merchants or middlemen and not – be it noted – by cutting back production. In its opening announcement, the cartel informed the world that amongst other things its intention was "to sell direct to consumers, and prices will be established in accordance with general business conditions as they develop from day to day". A uniquely one-sided attempt to resolve a many-sided problem and without recourse to the LME.

The exclusion of the LME was to be achieved first by the unilateral decision to reduce to a trickle sales to London merchants, and second by the establishment of an agency in Brussels to negotiate direct sales to European consumers. (US consumers were of course already tied – as to a great extent they still are – to the US domestic producers' price.) A further restriction was the limitation of tonnages sold to consumers outside the United States to what amounted virtually to their day-to-day needs only; in this way sale by a consumer of any surplus on the LME was minimised if not altogether prevented.

Stocks already in circulation on the market had of course to be acquired. These acquisitions were made not only by the cartel or its agents, but also by consumers anxious as to the availability of supplies at other than a monopoly price. (True, the first year or so of operation of Copper Exporters Incorporated had coincided with relative stability of prices.) As a result of these purchases, stocks in the United Kingdom fell from 50,000 tons in 1926 to fewer than 5000 in 1928. As is often the case when stocks are so drastically reduced, what little that does remain either is the less acceptable brands (rough copper for the most part in this instance) or is already well spoken for and so not truly free material.

The effects of the cartel's activity were both widespread and serious. The LME found its turnover dwindling away to a trickle, and consumers at the same time began to hanker after the freedom to bargain and to hedge their commitments which the market had previously afforded them. The monopoly was completely free to dictate prices as it chose (a delight which Secretan never quite achieved), and in October 1928 electro copper had risen to £75 per ton. All this was based on the withholding of supplies, on what amounted to almost daily partial *force majeure* declarations against selected consumers, and was indeed a very far cry from the pious sentiments quoted above.

But worse was to come. In 1929 (before the Depression and with trade still extremely active) the cartel yielded once and for all to the dictates of commercial greed in the face of extremely strong consumer demand. Prices were pushed higher yet and electro reached £114 per ton, with standard at a discount of £17 beneath this, along with secondary material recovered from scrap. At these levels, consumers began to withdraw from the market, and even some of the American members of the cartel became restive over not being permitted to dispose of cheaper grades (notably recoveries from scrap) at more competitive prices.

In the spring of 1929 Copper Exporters Incorporated yielded a little to pressure – largely from within its own ranks – and the export price was progressively reduced. Electro prices in London fell in sympathy first to £84. The initiative was still entirely with the cartel, however, and, as demand fell away with the beginnings of the Great Depression, there was no longer any pretence of a free market in copper.

The final break-up of the cartel was brought about in part by the appearance once more in the London market of rough copper refined from scrap, which was delivered against the standard contract. This movement spread to the point where custom-smelter members of the cartel began of their own volition to deliver some of what was fast becoming an embarrassing surplus to them. As these supplies came to the market, so prices began to fall towards something more in line with world economic conditions; and after a prolonged "high" at £84 in London electro fell to £66, and the US export price was cut once more.

This time, the liquidation – or assimilation by the market – of the vast surplus of stocks which had been amassed was not quite so tidy. Admittedly, this time such a liquidation had to be carried out in the face of a world depression of unprecedented seriousness. In the United States electro fell from 14 cents per pound in 1929 to 10 cents at the end of 1930 and then to an historic "low" in 1932 of 4 to 5 cents. In London, standard fell to its historic "low" of £25 per ton.

One interesting side-effect of this particular cartel operation was the stimulus it gave to some of the independent producers. Whilst American domestic production declined as a result partly of the slump but mainly because of distortion brought about by the manipulation of prices, those of Canada and Rhodesia were progressing strongly. At the same time the cartel had demonstrated – in spectacular fashion – the essential shortcoming of any such one-sided attempt at market control: lack of flexibility. It appears historically true, if at first sight illogical, that neither an entirely producer-controlled cartel (Copper Exporters Incorporated) nor an entirely consumer- or financier-directed one (Secretan) has the ability to stay close enough to, nor keep up with, changes in conditions in what is best described simply as the mood of the market. Inevitably it seems they lag, and they lack the breadth of perspective so essential in international marketing. It is these attributes – flexibility, speed, and breadth or catholicity of outlook – which merchants and brokers always have to offer.

There remains briefly to consider one further cartel operation, before examining the copper market in the years following the Second World War.

The blackest year of the Great Depression was 1932. By this time,

45

the copper market was effectively divided into two: the USA, which was virtually closed to imports by a high wall of tariffs, and the somewhat less restricted European markets. (The UK for example was then and still remains a free market as to import duties on copper from any source.) However, various political linings-up began to take shape, with Britain buying as far as possible from Empire sources, and France, Belgium and Germany all in varying degree associated with Katanga, Rhodesia and Eastern Europe. Chile and Peru were at the time marginal exporters only: though this situation was not to be a permanent one. Prices meanwhile remained low, with standard at or around £30 per ton or a little over.

In America, the very large unconsumed stocks were a continuing embarrassment. Restrictions had been placed on domestic sales from stocks, and a maximum quota also on sales from new production. Because of these restrictions, American producers had recourse only to the export market in order to divest themselves of at least some of their very heavy stocks, as well as to make over-the-quota sales of new output. Accordingly, American exports of copper rose from around 125,000 tons average to over a quarter of a million tons in 1934. Standard in London was further weakened to £25 12s 6d. It was clear that US selling, combined with increasing output from the "new" producers and the virtual collapse at the time of the important German market, were between them forcing copper prices to completely uneconomic levels. As an attempt to regularise trade in some way, the International Copper Cartel was set up in 1935.

The International Copper Cartel
Members of the new cartel agreed to restrict output to 75% of capacity from June of the year of its institution, and American exports were likewise to be pegged at 100,000 tons per year (lower than the average obtaining before the rise to 250,000 tons in 1934). Demand began to recover in 1935 and 1936, largely on rearmament programmes, and prices were held in a steady and unspectacular rise. Production and export quotas were progressively increased and, at around £35 per ton for standard, it began to appear as though equilibrium had been achieved at last.

But nothing remains static to the point of permanent equipoise in a world market in raw materials. In 1936 and early in 1937 there came one of those commodity booms which prove so difficult to attribute to any particular cause, and speculators on the bull tack came on to the market in some numbers. Once again prices started advancing, and once again the cartel was too slow in reacting to check the rise by increasing quotas; consumers predictably began to buy before the market rose too far against them. In March 1937 standard stood at £78 5s 0d.

By the time cartel quotas had been raised, and production increased to new levels, the buying boom had already ended. An unnecessary surplus situation had once more been brought about by the attempt (albeit a well-intentioned one) at control of the market in the teeth of supply and demand forces. Prices fell to about £40 per ton, and both production and export quotas were duly reduced once more. And, once more, too late to save the situation.

The copper market on the LME since the Second World War

Copper was the last of the four major metals to be returned to free market trading by the British Government after the war. Dealings actually recommenced on 5 August 1953 (and the market almost at once went into a backwardation, as its reopening coincided with a shortage of supplies).

The post-war scene in the world copper trade showed the main sources of production as Canada, Chile, the USA, the USSR, Zaire (Congo) and Zambia. New sources are, however, coming on stream at not infrequent intervals, and the Philippines and Bougainville are amongst these. Of the consuming countries Japan and West Germany emerged strongly as leading importers and refiners, while in the United States and the Russian bloc domestic production and consumption continue roughly to match each other.

The copper market continued to fluctuate: first downwards with the general running-down of the war machines of the belligerents; and later strongly upwards as industry (and notably the automobile industry) began to make heavy inroads on available supplies. As before, certain of the major producers began to look to fixed prices as a means of stabilising the market, and in 1955 the RST group initiated their own producer price to their customers, to be adjusted at intervals according to circumstances. (The other African Commonwealth producer, Anglo American, continued to base its prices on the LME.) But RST reverted to pricing on the LME after a couple of years, and the next move towards a producer or cartel price (outside the United States) was not to take place until 1961, when certain of the major producing countries established an agreed selling price of £234 per ton.

Before reviewing the progress of this latest attempt at a fixed-price system, it is worth noting that shortly before this time Japan came on to the scene for perhaps the first time in an international sense. In 1957 the Japanese Government permitted her nationals to make use of the LME for hedging purposes. Much aptitude was shown by Japanese industry in this field and it was not too long before a more direct connection was established. More than one LME member company now has a measure of Japanese shareholding, and the Japan Metal Centre was set up in London some few years ago as a further link.

To return to the producer price operation initiated in 1961, the countries participating were the African producers with Chile, but for various reasons their number excluded the United States, Canada and the USSR. The price rose from its original £234 by relatively easy stages to £236 in January 1966. This time, the price was proving to have been pegged too low – no doubt from concern regarding substitution for copper in various applications, notably by aluminium in the electrical field – and first Zambia and then Chile were persuaded to break away from the system. After a brief attempt at maintaining a producer price well in excess of that which had been the order of the day, Chile joined Zambia in the summer of 1966 in pricing on the LME three months quotation. Thereafter the LME became once more the medium, though the cash price was for a short time substituted for three months as the datum.

The three-tier copper contract on the LME

Introduction of the three-tier contract in July 1963 did not of itself prevent LME prices from rising well above those still fixed by the producers, and wirebars reached a high of £530 10s 0d in November 1964. They continued upward throughout 1965, and in April 1966 were priced at £787 10s 0d. It was at this point that the Chileans broke from the ranks of the producers' "club" and announced a selling price the equivalent of £496 sterling. This move was followed by the Zambian decision to revert to pricing their output on the much higher LME figure – though they based their quotations on three months rather than cash.

The divergence between the LME and the producer prices was largely the outcome of the fact that the free (LME) market was at the time too narrow, and therefore too easily subject to pressure. In this instance, buyers were anxious to ensure their marginal needs via the LME and they were understandably not too concerned about the price paid for what was a relatively minor proportion of a total intake the bulk of which was bought at an artificially low producer price. Once the producers, with the exception of those in the United States, reverted to pricing on the LME this situation no longer obtained and LME prices reacted downwards to less extreme heights and closer to the true value in terms of world supply and demand. The Americans remained wedded to producers' fixed prices, but it should be borne in mind that conditions in their domestic market were quite unlike those outside it. The United States was roughly in balance as to production and demand, and over her domestic market there hung the tonnage in the strategic stockpile, which could be released in tranches by the General Services Administration (GSA) on approval of Congress.

In 1967 the picture changed once more, when a major (and in the event prolonged) strike by copper workers in the United States broke out after failure of the triennial wage negotiations. The free market price began to climb as buyers hurried to ensure supplies for themselves before production was too severely cut back or even stopped altogether. The position as far as the LME was concerned was aggravated by the desire of American consumers now to buy on the world market, their domestic sources of supply having by autumn been cut by as much as 90% of smelting and 70% of refining capacity. That summer also saw heavy forward buying on the market in anticipation of a devaluation of sterling (one of the then British Government's worst-kept secrets). In the event, the pound sterling was devalued by some 14% on 18 November 1967, and the LME price of cash wirebars rose by roughly 10% from £502 to £556, indicating the extent of the discounting in advance which had taken place.

The strike in the United States continued. In early March 1968 record prices in excess of £840 were being offered for cash and a wide backwardation was ruling. But the signs were that the strike was at last coming to an end, as various individual plants settled fresh labour deals; at the end of the month cash wirebars had fallen to £620.

CIPEC

We have already seen something of the activities of more than one group which endeavoured with varying success to achieve some form of control over the market in copper. If "control" is too strong a word, then "stability" could be substituted, save that, in a worldwide market in an essential raw material which is very widely used, experience has shown that stability of price can be achieved only by a degree of control which amounts virtually to stifling the market altogether. Such control is both difficult to establish and usually impossible to maintain, as individual producer or consumer interests tend inevitably to go their own way when it suits them commercially to do so. It is not our purpose here, nor would it be proper, to moralise over this: we merely set it down as what appears to be true in the light of the evidence to date.

The CIPEC – Conseil International des Pays Exportateurs de Cuivre, to give it its full title – first came into being in 1967 with four members. These original members were Chile, Peru, Zaire and Zambia. CIPEC has a very different make-up and pursues a very different aim from the cartels we have already encountered. In the first place it is a grouping of countries with an interest in common as distinct from a grouping of commercial enterprises; this understandably puts it on a different footing altogether.

Faced with some fairly intractable problems – not least of which was the divergence in economic stamina and in political outlook between its original members – CIPEC has never gone further than to hold itself out as a primarily consultative body. New members and associate members have over the years broadened its scope and alleviated some of the early tensions between its founders in matters political. Yet it remains hard to see what such an organisation can actually do beyond providing a useful statistical and advisory service.

Other bodies have on occasion sought to modify the workings of the market in the cause of "stabilisation" of the price, but to very little real effect. The efforts, for example, of the UNCTAD Committee have been directed towards an altogether more grandiose proposition that there should be a form of overall "Common Fund" capable of building, financing and regulating stockpiles in all or any of a number of "core commodities". In the light of the difficulties experienced in conducting such an operation in a single commodity (within the International Tin Council and comparable bodies concerned with cocoa and coffee, for example) one finds it hard to be very sanguine about the prospects for the UNCTAD initiative.

The progress of the copper contracts
Both immediately before and during the period of the Secretan "corner", the LME authorities were being pressed by subscribers to

amend the copper contract with a view to broadening its base. This, it was held, would make it both more liquid in terms of volume and a far more efficacious hedging medium. Much of this pressure for a change was originating from consumers of physical.

The GMB contract

In response, there were some very significant changes made, the first in August 1888 with the institution of a contract for "Good Merchantable Brands" (GMB). This contract permitted delivery of a number of brands both of refined and of rough copper, provided that in every case the brand had been first registered with the Committee.

This new requirement has great significance in that it marked the beginning of the system of the authorisation of brands of metal by the Committee as a prerequisite of their acceptance as a good delivery. The formula adopted has stood the test of time remarkably well. Metal had then to assay not less than 93% copper, be certified as such by two independent and approved assayers and be spoken for as to suitability by two UK consumers. Today, virtually the only change has been in the raising of the required copper content in line with improved industrial techniques.

In addition, the contract specified a maximum forward trading period of three months for metal in warehouse in named delivery points (these at the time were Birkenhead, Liverpool, London and Swansea). Thus, the now traditional LME contract terms first became fixed.

The only drawback to the GMB contract was that it went perhaps too far along the hedging road in its catholicity, thus preventing consumers taking delivery under its terms with an embarrassment of assorted shapes and grades under the seller's option clause. This problem became more acute with the evolution of more advanced refinery processes: for example, fire-refined copper could be produced reliably at a guaranteed 99.75% Cu for "best selected", whilst tile copper could be produced assaying 99.25%. The final blow (though not an immediately fatal one) to GMB was the advent of electrolytic refining just before the turn of the century. This process enabled metal assaying as high as 99.9% to be produced, and by the end of the nineteenth century electro made up almost half the total supply. It was once more becoming apparent that the LME contract must be upgraded in line with technical progress outside, with GMB falling away to a proportion of the market comparable with that of the old Chile bar.

The standard copper contract

In January 1898 the Committee authorised the introduction of an additional contract to run alongside GMB. This new contract specified metal assaying 99.3% to 99.0% with the added refinement of a system of premiums for electro and discounts for rough down to 94.0%. Newcastle-upon-Tyne and Birmingham (an inland delivery point for the first and so far only time) were added to the list.

The GMB contract was to linger on for a further four years before standard became the sole copper contract – a position it was to occupy until 1963.

The three-tier contract

Known disrespectfully as the "Three-Ring Circus", this break with the past was made in 1963. Once again, the change was made in recognition of the changing scene in the production of copper and in the requirements of consumers. The method of accommodating grades of widely differing quality in one contract by authorising premiums and discounts is never perfect and by this time was becoming extremely clumsy in its application. It was therefore decided to split the contract three ways, and for each component to stand as a contract in its own right.

The first step was the rapid phasing-out of standard. Dealings for three months forward ceased at the beginning of July 1963 and no more dealings were sanctioned after these contracts became prompt at the beginning of September. The new contracts to replace standard were for wirebars, electro cathode and fire-refined copper. Of these types wirebars were in demand for drawing rod and wire down to the finest dimensions, whilst at the time cathode was used primarily for "pouring" – casting – and the constitution of alloys such as brass and bronze.

Of the three, fire-refined ceased to be priced officially after 1968, although the contract remains extant for such as care to use it; the wirebar contract was itself divided into electro and high-conductivity fire-refined (HCFR), which traded at a fixed discount below electro.

The higher-grade copper contract

During the later 1960s and early 1970s there had been intermittent debate on the LME as to the possibility of the cathode eventually superseding wirebars as a more or less universal copper shape for all manner of end-uses. Reports were coming in of the progress being made in the new continuous casting technique which made possible the drawing of rod and eventually fine wire from poured cathode. Hitherto this had been the preserve of the wirebar (and the origin of its name), which when heated to the correct degree of malleability could be fed through a series of rollers, each reducing the diameter of the rod so produced and increasing its length until considerable footage of unbroken wire of high electrical conductivity was generated. But there were difficulties, particularly in the heat control and the handling of the bar. And one break in the wire ruined it as an electrical product.

Continuous casting was a method of improving on the earlier processes. Here, cathode (or indeed almost any shape of the right quality) was first melted and then poured in a controlled stream into a groove in the periphery of a slowly revolving wheel. After following the wheel for one revolution, the rod so formed was sufficiently cool as to be fed directly into the first pair of rollers, for further reduction. Various patents were taken out – all based on the same basic concept – and the upshot was inevitable: a requirement for a greatly improved cathode as the first ingredient. One disadvantage of the standard of cathode then in production was that, owing to its greater surface area, it was more subject to blemishes and surface deformities than were wirebars.

Accordingly, it was decided to follow something like the path taken by the Tin Sub-committee in considering the introduction of a high-grade contract in that metal (see Chapter 6 on Tin). The outcome was the higher-grade copper contract which laid down that metal delivered might be either wirebars or cathodes of a better standard than hitherto. A list was drawn up of deliverable brands of higher-grade cathodes, to be added to the existing list of wirebar brands, for eligibility under the new contract.

Provision was made for a proportion of the cathodes in each parcel to be cut plates of a smaller size than their fellows (but not less than one quarter the size). There had always been problems with the bundling of cathodes and this concession was made in recognition of this fact, especially in the context of palletisation.

The future of the copper contract on the LME

In the autumn of 1973 the coincidence of the Yom Kippur War and of the violent and unexpected rise in the cost of energy brought a response in the form of a surge in the copper price until a peak was reached with cash wirebars at £1400 on 1 April 1974, accompanied by a backwardation of £191.

53

In the event, the effect of the startling rise in OPEC oil prices and of the temporary oil shortage caused by a partial embargo on supplies to Europe was not very long-lasting. After the initial shock the western economies reverted to type, and there were even signs of at least a sort of economic growth, despite the high level of inflation. This was not enough to maintain copper prices though, and the heady days of four figures for cash with a backwardation were soon in the past.

It was the second OPEC upheaval in 1978–79 which appears to have had the more profound, and to date more lasting, effect: it caused not, on this occasion, simply a "scare" reaction by consumers but the onset of a totally different economic weather-pattern. The depression which struck the western economies – if not such an emotive word, "slump" would have been a more accurate description – along with unprecedently high interest rates, notably in the United States, combined to depress, and to keep depressed, virtually all commodity prices. And the copper price has been amongst them.

The almost total lack of reaction to a series of upheavals which, traditionally, could have been expected to set commodity prices soaring is a phenomenon which is still being discussed and analysed by all concerned. Revolution in Iran, disturbances in Poland (a major producer of non-ferrous metals), the Gulf War and the invasion of the Falkland Islands seem to have been almost ignored by the markets. This is undoubtedly due to the depressant effect of high interest rates with their concomitant drawing of investment away from commodities into money, coupled with very high costs of capital investment in industry and of stockholding.

At all events, the situation is such that those who sought to control the copper market and stabilise prices – at whatever level seemed best to them – have other problems more pressing, including the shoring-up of economies, some of which look decidedly unsteady. It also remains to be seen to what extent the United States is to remain in a state of semi-isolation, or whether she will again come into the market as a force to be reckoned with.

Time alone will tell. What is moderately certain (and comforting) is that when the developed countries emerge from their economically suspended animation a resurgence in demand for copper is sure to follow. No doubt this will also reactivate the debate between the protagonists of the free market and those of control of commodity prices. Once again, as one of the most widely used and traded commodities, copper will be at the centre of the argument. It may well be that the LME's next preoccupation with the copper contracts will be on this rather than on a purely technical front.

6
Tin

Along with copper, tin was the subject of one of the original LME contracts. This may seem surprising, taking into consideration the claims of lead to be incorporated into LME trading: a less costly metal and one with many more sources of supply, most of which were closer to hand. However, the original purpose of the commodity markets was to facilitate trading in produce from the more remote sources overseas. It was probably this, coupled with tin's increasing importance in the nineteenth century as a constituent in pewter, bronze, white metal and other engineering amalgams, which provided the impetus for writing the first tin contract.

From their introduction into the LME to the present day these two "original" metals, copper and tin, have shown many divergent characteristics both as to price and as to sources of supply. Whilst sources of virgin copper have greatly increased in number and geographical spread from the early days of the Chile bar, those of tin have if anything become fewer. Today, the main areas of supply of tin metal and tin concentrates are those historic ones centred on the Malay Straits and the surrounding islands and countries, and Australia, Bolivia and, more recently, Nigeria. Curiously, the United States has little or no natural occurrence of tin. Sources in the United Kingdom are now to all intents and purposes out of the commercial picture, the once important Cornish tin-mining industry being but a shadow of what it once was.

Tin has a strategic importance to the extent that, as we shall see shortly, the United States saw fit during the Korean conflict to amass a considerable stockpile of it – a tonnage which has been hanging over a nervous market to greater or lesser degree ever since. Another peculiarity of this metal, and one which affects its supply, is the comparative scarcity of secondary tin recovered from scrap. There are technical reasons for this, bearing on the actual difficulties inherent in removing tin from steel in plated material, where, owing to its relatively high intrinsic value, the tin is laid on in an extremely thin coat.

All this tends to single tin out as in many ways a metal requiring much thought and not a little courage when trading on the Market. Indeed, the tin contracts on the LME are something of an "experts only" affair, involving larger sums of money than the others and a whole gamut of different and in the main political uncertainties.

Early history

The amalgamation of tin and copper to make bronze can be said to date from circa 3000 B.C., and Cornish production dates at least as far back as the first millennium B.C. The trading voyages of the Phoenicians from what is now Tunisia to Britain are well authenticated, and it is plain that this was already an established trade long before Julius Caesar's first expedition to Britain. It might well have been at least partly on account of knowledge of this profitable trade that the Romans came northwards at all and away from the area they already dominated.

Cornish tin was in mediaeval times associated with the Lamb and Flag brand mark. This constituted both a warranty as to purity and a confirmation that the King's dues had been met.The lamb carrying the flag is the emblem of the Knights Templar (who were the founders of the Inns of Court – Inner and Middle Temple – in London) and of the Knights Hospitaller, who possessed of the Norman and early Plantagenet Kings of England certain rights as to the sale of refined tin. For liturgical reasons, the brand mark was not universally acceptable – notably in Muslim countries – and after it had also been taken up by certain continental refiners it ceased to represent an exclusive trademark.

The importance to England of the production and trade in tin was reflected in the Charters granted by the Crown to the Stannaries, which gave a quite real measure of autonomy to certain towns in Cornwall, Devon and Somerset. (The curious history of the importance of tin to mediaeval and Tudor England is a study in itself, but is unfortunately out of place in the present context.) With the growth

57

of London as a trading and financial centre, the influence of the stannary towns declined, and control of the tin market passed into the hands of the Worshipful Company of Pewterers. It remained thus until the nineteenth century, when control was once more with the Cornish smelters and their agents. Marketing was by consignment of block tin from Cornwall to users or merchants in Bristol, Birmingham and London. Export was largely by way of London and Bristol merchants and the ubiquitous East India Company.

(In the latter part of the nineteenth century, exports and re-exports of tin amounted from a half to approximately three-quarters of home consumption.)

At this time, the import of tin from the East – the other major area of production – was inhibited by the imposition of a duty of no less than 60% *ad valorem*. In fact the average of imports between 1815 and 1830 amounted to only some 160 tons a year. By virtue of the Warehousing Act of 1823 it became possible to import and then re-export both tin and copper without attracting this extremely burdensome duty, and in consequence a brisk entrepôt trade in Australian and Straits tin was built up with the Continent of Europe. The higher purity of these brands, and their desirability in certain applications led to repeated approaches to the government by the tinplaters in Wales, and eventually to a progressive diminution of the tariff and to the birth of a significant import business in Eastern tin. As these uses of high-purity tin grew in volume, and notable amongst them was the expansion of the tinplating industry for which higher purity metal is essential, consumption of tin within the United Kingdom rose from some 6600 tons in 1860 to more than double that figure by 1875. By this time, too, actual import of block tin was roughly double the re-export figure, indicating a very considerable domestic market within the UK. The English merchants meanwhile had established a dominant position in the world tin trade, accounting then for some 50% of world production. Only the market in Amsterdam holding periodic auctions of Banka and Billiton tin offered any serious rivalry.

The tin market between the World Wars

After closure during the First World War, the market was re-opened for trading in December 1918 – remarkably soon after the cessation of hostilities – and prices began to fall rapidly from the levels reached during the war. The decline was short-lived though; the inexorable pull of inflation and depreciating currency values soon had prices climbing again. The trend was steepened by an appreciable amount of speculative buying for investment. In February 1920 tin at £419 had already surpassed its highest wartime price level. Within months, the reaction had set in, however, and in the early part of the following year the price of tin had fallen as low as £148. In industrial terms, the market was far from healthy: worldwide trade depression combined with a huge surplus of metal (either in stockpiles or in the form of now redundant items of ordnance) brought conditions which could only prove highly disadvantageous to the producing side of the metals industry. At about this period, the American and Chilean producers collaborated to form the Copper Export Association and a comparable operation in tin, the other major metal, was to be expected.

The Bandoeng Pool
In December 1920 the governments of the Dutch East Indies and of Malaya formed the Bandoeng Pool, with the intention of buying up surplus tin and so taking it off the market. During 1921 the pool did actually purchase some 19,000 tons; the decline in prices was reduced if not altogether halted, and this with only minor reductions in current production capacity.

Other influences were at work on prices, however, and the years before the return to the Gold Standard in 1925 were times of extreme currency fluctuations. The German Mark after reaching unplumbed depths collapsed in 1922 at 50 billion Marks per pound sterling, and even after the stabilisation of the Mark in 1924 there were fresh fears for the French franc. Speculators, or indeed anyone with money to husband, invested heavily in metals, or used the purchase and sale of metals or other commodities as a means for the transfer of paper money.

After these rather hectic years, comparative monetary stability was achieved with a general return to gold, this process being aided by the strengthening of the American economy, and the emergence in the United States of an industrial boom. (Unfortunately, these hopeful signs were not so manifest in Europe, with the United Kingdom, as an example, plunged into depression and a number of major strikes.) However, the international climate did become such that the Copper Export Association was wound up in 1924, and in the previous year the partners in the Bandoeng Pool began disposing of their stocks. This was carried out against a rising market in which consumption was now beginning to outrun production. So much so that when the disposals were completed in 1924 there was revealed the alleged "tin famine" – exaggerated perhaps, but real enough to bring about sharp and, in the event, lasting increases in prices.

This shortage brought fresh capital into prospecting and producing ventures. New mines and dredges were developed in Indo-China and Malaya and – significantly enough – in Nigeria, thus further demonstrating the extent of mineral reserves in the African continent. Mine output figures (overall) rose from 126,000 tons in 1923 to 196,000 in 1929, but by then signs were apparent of overproduction, and prices started to fall in sympathy. Voices began to be heard within the industry asking once again for some form of control of output in order to bolster up sagging prices. (In fact, the Anglo Oriental Corporation had already secretly withheld some of its production from the market with this aim in view.) The continuing decline in consumption in the years of the Great Depression made some form of restraint on production desirable if not actually essential.

The Tin Producers Association had been formed in 1929, largely as a forum for discussion, and this body now started endeavouring to persuade its members to restrict their own output on a voluntary basis. There was some response – which gave a measure of encouragement – but not sufficient seriously to assist in maintaining prices in the face of continuing oversupply. By the end of 1930, world tin stocks stood at 47,000 tons and the price was down to £112.

The International Tin Restriction Scheme
This was set up in 1931, and was organised at government level by the major producing countries, with the declared object of obtaining "a fair and reasonable relation between production and consumption [in order to] prevent rapid and severe oscillations in price". The scheme was to be worked according to a formula under which each member country would be allotted a standard tonnage, and its production based on a percentage quota of this amount. Quotas, which could be varied each quarter, were enforceable by the member governments. The membership of the schemes covered some 90% of world production capacity, with only China and the Congo as absentees amongst the larger producers.

The prospects for such a scheme were no doubt brighter in tin than in the other non-ferrous metals. There was (and remains) a far smaller element of scrap in tin than in copper and lead, for example;

and consumers in the main bought or stayed their hands more on current industrial conditions than on account of fluctuations in prices on the market.

The International Tin Committee was established as the governing body for the scheme, and commenced operations in March 1931. For the first year of operations, results were not very encouraging. However, the quotas were reduced in 1932 to one-third only of the standard tonnages, and prices began to turn upwards once more. Success fed upon success as stocks contracted – aided by the general increase in consumption of tin by industry – and prices in fact reached the comforting figure of £230 per ton by the end of 1933. This from a level of £118 in 1931, the first year of the scheme's operation.

The Tin Buffer Pool
The scheme was reinstated in 1934 for a further three-year period; that year quotas were increased yet remained below consumption with stocks declining to less than 20,000 tons. The average price was held at £230. In point of fact, an artificial shortage had been brought into being. Observing this, the International Tin Committee took the decision to establish a buffer pool of tin which could itself be expanded or contracted as a means of effecting a finer and more rapidly responsive adjustment than the somewhat crude method of restrictions on production. In a falling market the pool would buy surplus metal, which it would be in a position to sell on the market once more in case rising consumption (or speculative activity) were seen to be forcing prices too high.

The proposal to set up the buffer pool was not at the time universally welcomed. There were many who felt that the position had been brought sufficiently under control for it to have been an unnecessary subtlety. There were also objections to maintaining the price as high as £230 per ton, such a figure being held to be an encouragement to the continuance of high-cost production (being now profitable at such price levels) at the expense of further development of lower-cost and arguably more efficient operations. Consumers naturally saw the development as yet another strengthening of the producers' already close hold on the market, to no discernible benefit to themselves or their interests.

The reaction of the LME was both hostile and swift. Alarmed at the deleterious effect on the market of the transfer of all power of decision to the Buffer Pool Manager of the International Tin

Committee, the Board of the Exchange sent a sharp protest to the British Colonial Office, in which they roundly condemned the whole concept as being against the interests of a free and open market.

Notwithstanding these hostile reactions, the pool was formally established in July 1934, supplies going directly into it from members of the International Tin Agreement. The pool started life therefore with some 8000 tons of tin to its name. Members of the agreement meanwhile continued to look kindly on the formation of "private" stock pools, and the International Tin Committee continued to buy metal from all comers when the market price fell below £230. The buffer pool itself did not trade in its early months, as quotas were still restricted to 40% of standard tonnages and by the end of 1934 world stocks were down to only 19,000 tons.

The situation grew progressively more acute in the following year. Supplies of visible tin in the United Kingdom fell to "starvation" levels with the inescapable result that a wide backwardation appeared. In fact, the shortage of tin for delivery had the effect of virtually stopping the LME from functioning at all: the backwardation made hedging an impossible business, and deliveries to and from the market were reduced to a trickle. (An extensive backwardation invariably has this unfortunate effect on hedging, since covering-in places the hedger at the mercy of the "back".) Both the LME and the consuming and merchant trades continued to protest, without at the time persuading the International Tin Committee to increase supplies to the market. By way of a demonstration of their disapproval and frustration, it is reported that the LME dealers walked out of the tin Ring on one occasion!

It would appear that communications at the time between the ITC and the Exchange could not have been of the best. The ITC maintained that the LME was "a playground for both bulls and bears", and that sales of cash tin on the market were nothing more than the result of bear speculation. In perspective, it would seem less than likely that a speculator in such market conditions would put himself in the position of an uncovered bear: the sales were almost certainly genuine hedging. However, the ITC were not convinced. The tin market on the LME remained in considerable disarray throughout 1935. On 22 July, for example, bidders in the Ring for cash tin pushed their bids up from £236 to £245 without attracting a single seller. Further protests were made to Whitehall, to be countered by the rather baffling rejoinder that (though Britain was a member of the ITC) HM Government accepted no responsibility for the policy of the manager of the buffer pool. Reassurances were, however, given – apparently contradicting the disclaimer – that the pool would be so administered as not to interfere with the normal workings of the Exchange. But stocks of tin in Liverpool and London remained at precariously low levels (to a low, in November, of 300 tons as compared with a usual average of around 5000 tons), and the wide backwardation continued.

The ITC did, however, respond to the situation they had themselves largely created by raising production quotas twice in the course of 1935 – ultimately to 90% of the standard tonnages. In the following year, stocks in the United Kingdom began to assume less desperate levels and the Exchange responded with a narrowing backwardation. However, 1936 continued on an unsettled course. There were uncertainties about the likely renewal of the scheme (and what form it might take), there were difficulties over the continued membership of Thailand, and these were reflected in widely fluctuating prices after a sharp break that summer. The third International Tin Agreement was in fact signed at the end of 1936 with prices once more in excess of £230.

In the following year, 1937, world trade was again on the ascendant, and the combined requirements of a considerable boom and heavy rearmament programmes brought huge increases in demand. In March, prices touched £311, the buffer pool was exhausted of tin and production quotas were duly raised as high as 110% of the standard tonnages. In the closing months of the year there was a general decline in production which was to continue throughout 1938. At the time, there was a recession in the United States, and this was to prove the major influence on the market. Prices again began to waver and then to fall: eventually to below £200 per ton. The market was further upset that year by a spate of rumours of the formation of a new buffer pool.

The second tin buffer pool was brought into operation in June 1938. Once again, it was stocked initially by tin provided by members of the agreement rather than by purchases in the market. The innovation on this occasion was the establishment of the concept of a range of prices which would dictate the limits of permitted activity on the part of the manager. In this instance, he might sell or buy in order to contain prices within the band £200 to £230 per ton. Again, there was outspoken opposition to the scheme, including the accusation of adding price-fixing (within narrow limits) to the existing catalogue of producer-controlled restrictions of a free market.

Indeed, since the London price at the time was but £188 it did appear that the producers were merely seeking protection for themselves at the expense of consumers. Speculators, too, foresaw the possibility of a rise in price and started their operation with this in view; and numerous private "pools" were set up by purely speculative interests.

During the year production quotas were again reduced, with the consequence that supplies became short once more. However, as prices rose to £230 in 1939 the buffer pool accordingly began to offer tin to the market. But the Second World War was imminent: demand rose strongly and the UK Government itself intervened to peg the London price at a maximum of £230, and to introduce a system of export licensing in order to conserve strategic supplies. For a time, the free market shifted to New York, and prices there rose from the equivalent of £229 per ton in August to £331 in the following month. By the end of August 1939 the buffer stock was virtually exhausted, production quotas were increased, and any serious attempt at control over the market was placed in abeyance. With the removal in December of the official price ceiling in the United Kingdom, London prices (once more free) averaged around £249.

These attempts at control appeared to have suffered from many of the shortcomings which afflicted similar operations in copper, and to have brought in their train very comparable side effects. What was to emerge and develop in the years after the war?

The tin market since the Second World War

Being primarily a sterling commodity, tin did not present the same exchange problems as did the markets in the other metals. In addition, production of tin in the early post-war years was already running ahead of consumption, thus refuting any argument for the continuation of government rather than free market buying. There remained some risk of loss of foreign exchange resulting from commodity "shunting", but such losses could occur only where there existed unofficial markets in transferable sterling which was offered at a discount below official parity. This risk was greatly reduced by the devaluation of the pound sterling in September 1949.

At the end of September the UK Government announced the termination of bulk purchasing contracts for tin, and, with the exception of the disposal of remaining stocks, Government intervention in the market could cease. Accordingly, 15 November 1949 saw the re-opening of the tin market: the first of the LME markets to be freed after the end of the war.

The Bank of England Metals Scheme
Dealings still had to be accommodated within the framework of exchange control regulations and requirements, however, and, in order to ensure this, arrangements were worked out by the Bank of England and the Committee of the LME acting in close co-operation. The general tenor of these arrangements is covered on later pages and the scheme is mentioned here in order merely to establish its place in the chronological order of developments.

Since rubber was the only other London commodity market already re-opened, the recommencement of tin dealings on the LME excited much interest and comment in business circles worldwide. Its success or otherwise was seen to be a reliable indicator of the likely success of other markets, and, indeed, of the concept of free markets generally in the economic world now emerging. In all, the successful re-opening, after a long period of scrupulously careful preparation, of the first of its markets was a very real fillip to the whole image and morale of the LME.

One major problem remaining was how best to ensure the orderly disposal of the country's strategic stocks of tin. The Committee of the LME were as one in the opinion that any such disposals should be done by way of sales in the market, on the standard contract. It was proposed that one broker be charged with responsibility for the sales and by agreement with the Ministry of Supply Mr J. D. Wolff (Chairman of the Committee) was appointed in this capacity. A nice touch was the agreement within the Exchange that commission received be pooled for sharing equally amongst the Ring members! To start with, the market was almost wholly dependent upon the "Government Broker" for its chips in terms of cash metal, and balanced stocks were only built up with some difficulty as other warrants began to make their appearance. Prices at the outset fell noticeably, indicating an over-valuation of tin in the years without a free market. The Ministry's last official quotation had been £750, but by 25 November – 10 days after the market re-opened – standard had fallen to £642 10s 0d cash, and at year's end to barely £600. At first there was a considerable backwardation as the direct reflection of a lack of stocks; but this had given way to a narrow contango in March 1950 as conditions became more stable and stocks were being built up. All was indeed proceeding very smoothly, until the outbreak of hostilities in Korea in June 1950. Immediately, buying developed on a very large scale and an acute shortage was seen to be approaching very rapidly. Fears were based on two main grounds: first the general human tendency to stockpile in time of crisis, and second quite well-founded fears of a spread of hostilities severely disrupting shipping to and from the East and the transit of such supplies as remained on offer. The United States led the way with massive purchases for her own stockpile, and other nations followed suit: there was also the predictable scramble by speculators to come into what was now a rapidly rising market.

The market in fact rose in an unprecedented manner. From averaging around £600 per ton from the start of dealings until early 1950, cash tin reached £800 by mid-August and £1300 in November. On 14 February the high point was reached of no less than £1615 per ton, with three months at a considerable backwardation. A far cry from the immediately pre-war support price of £200–£300. An unfortunate effect of this heavy buying by relatively few purchasers was the dependence of others on rumours of their intentions and forthcoming activities, and the consequent erratic behaviour of the market – with daily fluctuations as great as £100. In the United Kingdom the Ministry of Supply became alarmed at the shortage of stocks, and announced in August that it could no longer be depended upon as a willing seller of cash. However, stocks on warrant totalled only a nominal 100 tons, shipments from the East were, in the event, gravely disrupted and the Ministry was compelled to make sales from time to time in order to keep the market open at all. This it did on condition that members themselves operated a self-imposed ban on sales for export. The seemingly relentless upward pressure on prices under these conditions was the subject of much worried discussion and negotiation, as government and other agencies sought some form of agreement to limit what had degenerated into a scramble for supplies at virtually any price. The rise could only be, and in the event was, stopped by the removal of its root cause. The by now enormous cost of stockpiling finally persuaded Congress in the United States to stage a dramatic alteration of course. In a report, a Committee of Congress had accused producers of "gouging" the US taxpayers by failing to increase output to meet vastly increased demand. (As this increase in demand could be said to be exceptional, and in all probability of limited duration, it is rather hard to see the justice of such an accusation. What would have happened later to the surplus capacity which might thus have been brought on stream?) The US Administration then decided to discontinue stockpile purchases until prices had fallen "to a reasonable level". In March, the Reconstruction Finance Corporation (RFC) was authorised as the sole importer into the USA, and even usual commercial purchases were suspended on the grounds that producers were asking too much for their metal or concentrates. Controls were at the same time placed upon consumption within the USA.

Tin now found itself in surplus once more, and prices in London fell almost as fast as they had risen, falling to £867 in July 1951. Throughout this whole cycle, the LME traded without interruption or embarrassment to any member. For the ensuing two years, and no doubt to the relief of those concerned, the tin market passed through a period of quite remarkable tranquillity. Average prices in fact varied between a minimum of £948 and a maximum of £984 in the period January 1952 to March 1953. This even tenor of prices was not the outcome solely of free-market dealing, however. The RFC had entered into fixed-price purchasing agreements with the governments of the Congo, Indonesia and the United Kingdom, and this enabled it to be a seller at a consistent £964 (121.5 cents per lb). Originally a floor price, the figure became the ceiling price after August 1952 when normal commercial imports into the USA were resumed. London prices continued to follow the RFC as supplies from other sources were still insufficient to meet demand, which had perforce to lean heavily on RFC sales. The situation persisted until early 1953, when prices started again to break. The RFC's purchasing contract was shortly to terminate and it was felt that a surplus would result; in addition there was a slackening of international tensions with the cessation of hostilities in Korea. In July 1953 the London price fell to £567. Although in retrospect these two years had been years of stability as to prices in London, this very stability had impeded the equally necessary hedging and speculative activity on the market.

There had also been a resuscitation of commodity shunting activity due to the weakness of transferable sterling. Merchants on the Continent were able to take advantage of cheap transferable sterling rates and so buy tin in London and Singapore for sterling, sell it at "cut price" terms for US dollars in New York and still show a profit on the exchange conversion. It was intimated that some 30,000 tons of Straits tin found a home in the United States by this route, costing the United Kingdom some $80,000,000 in dollar reserves. At the request of the Bank of England, the Committee of the LME appealed to members to be chary of taking business from doubtful sources and in particular to check carefully any terms in contracts for "on-shipment" with clients outside the United Kingdom. At the same time, the authorities in Malaysia co-operated by requiring certificates from purchasers of Straits tin confirming that the material had been consumed in the country to which it had been consigned, and not "shipped on".

The only real cure for this as for so many problems, however, could be the removal of its true cause, in this case the difference between official exchange rates for sterling and the unofficial rates. In early 1953 the Exchange Equalisation Account took the decision to support the exchange rate on dealings in overseas markets and thus keep it so close to the official rate that discount dealings were no longer profitable. Whilst this disparity in rates for sterling brought about technical disparities between tin prices in London, Singapore and New York (which were normally, and ought to be, in harmony), it also had an adverse effect on the business of the London dealers who were unable to take advantage of cheap sterling rates in order to meet competition in the New York market as to the dollar price there.

The Penang market – "The East"

Those who follow metal prices without actually being involved in physical trading may be excused for a certain feeling of mystification at the mention of tin prices in "The East". This cryptic reference is to the cash market in physicals in Penang off the coast of Malaysia.

Here, the two major smelters in the area daily conduct a spot market in tin and in concentrates which can then be smelted into saleable metal in their furnaces. The amount to be offered each day depends on their intake from the producers, many of whom are small independent mines with limited output, and bids are matched against available supplies.

Should the total of bids on any day exceed that of supplies, the allocations to bidders are rationed; should the declared price be higher than that of some of the bids on which it was based, then the whole of that day's intake need not be disposed of. Delivery of metal ex-smelter is usually up to 60 days after pricing and there is no facility for forward trading. In consequence, hedging must be done on the LME. The Penang market is very largely a one-way affair, since restrictions are enforced against resale of metal purchased.

The International Tin Agreements
Though far from being an unqualified success, the series of International Tin Agreements of which each has a five-year duration deserve mention as being arguably the closest which has yet been achieved towards a genuine bilateral marketing arrangement with both producing and consuming interests having a voice.

A child of the United Nations, the first ITA was drawn up in 1956 after preliminary work by the International Tin Study Group. The International Tin Council, with offices in London, was made up of representatives of both producers and consumers. A Buffer Stock Manager was appointed, and to the old "range" of the pre-war buffer pools were added three ranges between floor and ceiling prices. Originally the Buffer Stock Manager was obliged to sell tin when prices exceeded the ceiling and could sell at discretion when they were in the upper range. He had to remain inactive when prices were in the neutral range, could buy when they were in the lower range and had to buy when they "fell through the floor". Subsequent ITAs have varied this procedure to include being an overall net seller or buyer, and being a lender or a borrower on the LME.

The Buffer Stock Manager operates both on the LME and in the Penang market, where he is privileged to be both a buyer and a seller. Prior to the decision to allow sterling to "float" at the termination of the Bretton Woods system of fixed currency parities, the ITA price range was quoted in sterling per tonne. Since that time it has been quoted in Malaysian ringgits, first per picul (a local measurement of weight) and later per kilogramme. The Penang prices, too, are expressed in ringgits per kilo, with the result that a foreign exchange conversion is necessary for dealings in sterling. He may operate through any member of his choosing, though the story that at one time he chose them in alphabetical order is probably apocryphal. (It was claimed that after member *A* had executed an order for the Buffer Stock Manager the next in line was certain to be member *B*, with the consequence that fellow members were in a position to lie in wait for him on the Ring.)

One of the many problems facing the ITC has been the existence of the US Strategic Stockpile, which on occasion looms over the market like a threatening cloud. The fact that the US was not a member of the ITA meant that, though he could deal with stockpiles held in member countries, the Buffer Stock Manager had no voice in dealing with what was and remains the largest of them all. This huge reserve (at one time exceeding 250,000 tons) was built up by the General Services Administration as controller of all US strategic materials during the Korean War. Releases are made from time to time: for example in 1964 no fewer than 28,994 tons were disposed of, equal then to five weeks' average world tin consumption.

With or without the overhanging US stockpile, the lot of the Buffer Stock Manager has not been a totally happy one. From time to time he has found himself strapped either for money when buying to support a sagging price or for metal when endeavouring to sell in order to keep the price within reasonable bounds. In this context, and as a comparison with today's prices of about ten times that amount, he was "lost to view beneath a mountain of tin" (to quote a distinguished LME member) as early as 1958, when buying to support a price of £730 per ton! In 1963 the reverse happened twice: first when a spate of Russian buying pushed the price through the ceiling and later when cash once more passed the £965 "must sell" figure and the Buffer Stock ran out of tin.

This uncomfortable progress will almost certainly continue to be the lot of successive Tin Agreements and Buffer Stock Managers. As we have already noted, the world's sources of tin are few, and some are situated in highly sensitive areas, for example Vietnam, the Congo area and Korea.

Add to this the difference in outlook and in economic aims of members of successive ITAs – to say nothing of the political considerations inherent in deciding whether or not to become a member at all – and it can readily be seen that this exercise in international marketing strategy is far from easy to carry out. Nevertheless, and despite a further massive squeeze on the LME tin market in the early months of 1982, the International Tin Agreements bid fair to remain a permanent part of the scene. The tin market has a history of such endeavours at achieving stabilisation; it is only fair to say that the development of the ITA concept has to date been by a big margin the one coming closest to success.

The early contracts

The first tin contracts on the LME contained much the same provisions as those for copper, in terms of deliveries and prompts. As was natural, the contracts were amended in the light of experience from time to time, with the difference being that unlike the market for copper, where increasing consumer demand had to be catered for, the Exchange had continually to maintain its endeavours to safeguard this rather thin market from being squeezed. This proclivity remains a factor in the tin market today.

From the outset the contractual tonnage for tin was set at 5 tons, and at first deliveries were confined to London.

Good Merchantable Quality (GMQ)
In 1891 the early contracts were superseded by a single GMQ contract. By permitting only the delivery of Australian and Straits tin, however, this contract was to prove too narrow for hedging purposes even though it met the needs of those seeking physical deliveries.

Mixed tin
In 1897 therefore, a second contract for mixed tin was introduced which included Banka and Billiton tin as good delivery. The effect of this move was that GMQ remained the chief delivery contract whilst hedging was done largely on mixed.

Unfortunately, this addition to the range of deliverable tin was not sufficient to prevent continued attempts to corner the market. Legend has it that one LME firm, Messrs Ricard and Freiwald, became expert in this by strategic movement of the partners' yacht, ballasted with tin in lieu of the traditional pig lead.

The Committee were in due course approached with a view to their taking steps to prevent or at least inhibit such manipulation of the tin market. This taxed them with the difficult choice of allowing complete freedom in dealings on the market – one of the most basic principles of the LME – or of restricting any dealings which might be held to be endangering the market's equilibrium. In the event, the Committee opted for the latter course, as much to preserve the Exchange's reputation in the eyes of the world as for any other reason, and a new rule was adopted in 1899. This rule gave the Committee the right to release members from their market commitments to deliver warrants against outstanding contracts where it had been established that an "Oppressive Corner" was in being. Under this rule, prompts could be extended or effected at a predetermined settlement price. Unfortunately, in practice the rule was not altogether effective as at first framed, since it could then be invoked only at the behest of 12 members; in 1911 the Committee were authorised to invoke it on their own initiative. The rule still stands in the current Rules and Regulations as Contract Rule "H", and it gives the Committee the power if they think a corner is being established to "investigate the matter and to take whatever action it considers proper to restore equilibrium between supply and demand . . .". Practice is never as easy or as precise as theory, however, and the risk of being held to be oppressing one or more members to the benefit of others is a severe deterrent to the taking of any such drastic action. In actual fact, operation of the rule is by way of a quiet word with the offender in the majority of the infrequent cases of its being invoked at all.

The Committee still looked towards broadening the scope of the contract as the best means of achieving a more truly representative market. To this end, they were in 1911 considering admission as good delivery of English ingot and of Chinese and German tin at seller's option, but the proposal was resisted by those members who represented consumers. These latter argued that the admission of inferior grades would worsen the position by driving users towards direct dealings with producers and so bypassing the LME, an argument which, with the benefit of hindsight, can be said to have had a lot of merit.

The standard tin contract

This was introduced in 1912, in the face of strong opposition, in a further attempt to solve the intractable problem of supplies in a narrow market. Under this contract, sellers might deliver Class A tin of Australian or Straits origin, or refined tin assaying not less than 99.75% Sn. Class B tin was the alternative – and the innovation – in that it included common tin from English and other suppliers assaying down to a permitted minimum of 99% Sn. This latter was to be deliverable at a discount of £7 below the contract price.

Opposition to the new contract reached the point where some members refused to trade in it and confined their activities to GMQ; the difficulty was only partly resolved by the introduction in 1913 of a CIF contract for certain named grades, which were sold at buyer's option on shipment terms. The effect of these attempts at rationalising the market was to drive the greater part of physical trading away from the Ring, which became a hedging and from time to time a speculative medium.

All in all, the tin market on the LME was very volatile, and very prone to distortion during these years leading up to the First World War. Prices could range in the course of one year from a high of £200 to a low of £115, and from £233 to £169 – all too easily understandable in a narrow market with insufficient geographical (and economic) spread as to its sources of supply. Malayan prices tended to fluctuate widely, and they were those on which exports from the East were priced. Sales of Banka in Amsterdam were periodic, and resulted in periodic surges of supply in the West. The market was in fact passing through an unhappy phase of great vulnerability, and was the subject of more than one cornering attempt by numerous syndicates, of which Secretan has already been noted in connection with copper. In 1888 the Secretan Syndicate withdrew from the tin market (they were to hold out a little longer in copper), and prices in London promptly fell from £166 on 27 April to £80 on 4 May in that year.

As to the standard contract itself, further changes have been made in the continuing effort to maintain a balance between a broad hedging contract and one which is sufficiently precise as to enable a consumer to take up the desired grade of actual metal against it. By the mid 1920s there was enough physical demand for the Class B brands to allow the discount on English tin to have been all but eliminated in dealings done outside the market. Accordingly, official discounts were reduced first to £5 in 1925, and 10 years later to £4. In 1935 also the minimum purity requirement was lowered from 99% Sn to 98.5% in order to include the increasing volume of Chinese tin which was by then being traded in both the UK and America. There was a fixed discount of £7 in the case of this lower-grade metal.

By 1958 the contract was amended once more, this time to exclude common tin. At this date, metal had to be either Class A1 (named brands, including English refined tin) or A2, being other tin of good merchantable quality assaying not less than 99.75%. Both A1 and A2 were deliverable at the contract price. Later still, the standard contract crystallised as to quality requirements, stipulating a purity of not less than 99.75% and that the metal be "of a brand approved by and registered with the Committee". The naming of individual brands on the contract had been discontinued.

The high-grade tin contract

By the early 1970s it was becoming apparent that the standard tin contract was losing some of its authority. There was at the time a general shortage of 99.75% tin, owing in part to the closure of one of the UK's major smelters, and in consequence a growing proportion of higher-grade metal was being traded against the standard contract at varying premiums. Some LME members had acquired considerable expertise in conducting a form of arbitrage in warrants and premiums; for a time they were not enthusiastic about introducing a new high-grade contract, no doubt for good commercial reasons. More seriously, an increasing volume of trade was known to be by-passing the LME altogether.

A sub-committee was set up to look into the matter, and its members' thinking first led them in the direction of a reintroduction of the erstwhile practice of defining deliverable metal by naming brands, but in the event this line was not pursued. Instead, it was recommended that a new contract for high-grade tin assaying not less than 99.85% Sn be introduced to run alongside the standard contract. Producers of 99.85% were invited to offer their brands for registration and their response was encouraging: clearly some if not all of the producers had not relished having their metal traded at premiums over LME standard which were not of their making. The Buffer Stock Manager of the ITC was kept *au fait* with developments and he, too, gave the new contract his blessing.

With this encouragement, the new high-grade contract was approved by the Board and full Committee and instituted in August 1974 for prompts on and after 1 November that year, allowing the usual three months for stocks to build up before deliveries under the contract commenced. After a somewhat hesitant start, with dealings in both contracts taken together in the same Ring, a pattern began to emerge, with premiums for high-grade apparent, at any rate in the forward months.

There are those who, on considering the performance of the new contract, have reservations as to its success. Certainly it must have given the protagonists of a higher-grade zinc contract food for thought. In a sense, the high-grade tin contract serves to highlight the eternal conundrum on any futures market: whether to cater for the consumer with his precise requirements, or the hedger and speculator who are best suited by a totally standard deliverable product, which for the most part they do not need to see delivered, their aim being to establish a price only.

The outlook

The future of the tin contracts on the LME is somewhat shrouded in mystery. As we have seen, conditions on the supply side are such as to make the market a thin one and highly vulnerable to squeezing. At the same time, consumption overall is not likely to decline significantly despite inroads made notably by aluminium in canning.

New uses for tin seem to be almost without limit. It has to be allowed, however, that it is, and is likely to remain, a highly political metal – with all that implies.

Despite occasional upheavals, such as the upward pressure on prices for cash in the early months of 1982 which was followed by an abrupt fall to an appreciable discount below Penang, the contract remains an important one for trade hedging in a very expensive metal. There is also a measure of speculation in tin – its very volatility makes the contract attractive – but this is confined for the most part to an expert few who have the feel for this very individual market.

7

Lead and Zinc

The situation as to lead and zinc on the LME is very different from that of the other metals. Both are found in some abundance in Europe and the mining and smelting of European ores contributes to a sizeable overall production of refined metal. Britain herself was an exporter of lead in earlier times, though increasing industrialisation in the eighteenth and nineteenth centuries later reversed the picture, as had been the case with English tin. The main areas of British production were located in the Pennines (with Chesterfield as a marketing centre), the Mendips and the Welsh Mountains. After the Union of the two countries, Scottish output from Lanarkshire and the Central Lowlands was added. Production from these mines was for the most part smelted locally, and shipments for exports sailed from Bristol, London, the Tyne and the South Wales ports.

Along with Germany and Spain – though a larger producer than either – the United Kingdom thus remained one of the world's leading producers of lead until the latter part of the nineteenth century. However, at this time the somewhat fragmented mining industry in the UK began to give way before continental competition, and in 1870 both Germany and Spain surpassed the British output of lead. Before the turn of the century the United States in her turn surpassed all others to become the world's premier producer. (At the same time, however, mining operations were getting under way in Australia and Mexico amongst other areas, and these countries, too, were in due course to become important centres of production.)

By the 1880s, therefore, Britain was established as an importer of lead to the tune of some 100,000 tons per annum of pig and sheet and more than 16,000 tons of ore. Imports by that time already amounted to over three times her own domestic production. It is worth noting though that an entrepôt trade in lead was developing as well: in 1885 this onward business totalled almost 40,000 tons.

As to zinc (or spelter as it was known until after the First World War), production had largely been concentrated in Europe; and by the middle of the nineteenth century the region of Upper Silesia was the chief producing area. Smelting was for the most part carried out in Belgium and Germany, at first with European ores only, although later imported ores and concentrates were used as the industry grew rapidly to very large figures. The USA, too, was a producer of zinc, but being to a great extent self-supporting as to raw materials (with the exception of tin) her output was for the most part used in her own domestic consumption.

During the nineteenth century, both the production and the trade in zinc as they affected the LME were centred on, and largely controlled from, the Continent. Commodity exchanges were in fact established in various European locations (and not only for dealings in metals), the Hamburg Metal Exchange being opened in 1910. This particular market achieved a considerable importance in dealings in lead and zinc in the relatively brief period before its closure in 1914. Most European exports to Britain were unloaded in Hull and in London. There was at the time but little entrepôt business in zinc, and market activity in London was almost exclusively confined to physical dealings by merchants in respect of UK consumption.

This predominance of Germany in the lead and zinc fields was to a very great extent attributable to the success of a few major enterprises, amongst them being Metallgesellschaft of Frankfurt. These organisations spread their interests widely in terms both of geography and of the various stages of production from mining through to marketing the refined metals. (Indeed, the whole Spanish mining industry was then very dependent on German investment.) Metallgesellschaft was later to build itself into a position of particular importance, and it is of more than passing interest to observe that this organisation – which was founded in the 1860s by the Merton brothers – is a Ring dealing member of the LME through its London company.

The LME and the contracts before the First World War
Dealings in lead and zinc were for the most part confined to a

77

relatively few members, and were conducted outside the main Ring. This was not necessarily due to lack of interest in these metals but to the fact that they were not at the time (nor indeed for some years to come) sold on the basis of a transferable warehouse warrant giving title to a parcel of stocks in warehouse. It was not then possible to conduct hedging business in lead or zinc: deliveries were ex-ship and for cash against bills of lading or delivery orders. There were wide variations in the purity of metal supplied, and this factor did not make the setting of a standard contract-unit of material any easier. The two factors combined to restrict almost entirely to physical dealings a market where as yet there was no formalised contract and there were no freely transferable documents of title such as were in use for dealings in copper and tin.

The good soft pig lead contract was introduced in 1903 and was the outcome of much discussion in the endeavour to arrive at a formula which would make it feasible for lead to be bought and sold forward in the same way as tin and copper. The contract made no attempt to limit deliverable grades to a list of approved brands, as it was not felt necessary for consumers to be so specific in their choice of material. Warehouse warrants were still not used, and deliveries continued to be ex-ship or ex-wharf in the Thames between Nine Elms and Tilbury: the Port of London Authority area. Later, a system of discounts admitted deliveries further down-river.

An ex-ship delivery, rather than one from stock already in warehouse, meant uncertainties as to completion dates. The new contract was in this sense more akin to those in use on the "soft" commodity markets in that it provided for a delivery month (rather than a prompt date) up to three months ahead. A further period of grace of 15 days was allowed to the seller, in the event of the delayed arrival of a ship.

With all its looseness, and consequent shortcomings as a really viable hedging medium, the new contract was a success. Indeed, it survived with surprisingly little change up to quite recent times.

A comparable contract for virgin spelter was introduced in 1915, with delivery points extended to include Liverpool (ex-quay or ex-warehouse) and Swansea (free on rail (FOR)).

Producer cartels before the First World War

The concentration of the lead and zinc industries in relatively few areas (and in relatively few pairs of hands) made conditions much less unfavourable for the establishment of producer cartels than had been the case with either copper or tin. Outside the United States, which being self-sufficient at the time was largely isolated from the rest of the world trade, the main smelters were located in Belgium and Germany and to a lesser degree in Britain and France. Ownership of many of these smelters furthermore was confined to a few organisations and the cartel "rationale" generally was both established and indeed encouraged in Germany.

Throughout the last decade of the nineteenth century there were repeated rumours in circulation about a potential zinc cartel and they were sufficiently strong to have an unsettling effect on prices. At the time, the industry was labouring under difficult conditions of low prices combined with high raw material costs: some form of co-operation on the part of the producers therefore appeared to be a strong possibility. In the event, however, the producers were unable to agree on a combined plan for restriction of output, the rumours began to be discounted and prices to recover. The notion of a producers' cartel was not revived until 1908 in fact, when the German industry approached groups in Belgium, Britain and France with the result that in 1909 the European Spelter Convention was set up.

The aim of the Convention was the control of production, and each producer member agreed to abide by a quota which would be reduced if stocks rose to more than 50,000 tons or the London price fell below £22 per ton. (There was no attempt made at actually fixing prices.) As happened with comparable cartels in other metals, the Convention's early years appeared successful, to the extent of its renewal in 1911 for a further three years. (It is interesting to speculate on the exact cause and effect of these parallel situations. Would things have been otherwise had there been no cartel – since action was not in the event demanded of it – or did its very existence in some way and for a limited time so restrain disruptive forces as to maintain an orderly market almost in spite of itself?) In any case, the years 1911 and 1912 were happy ones for the European zinc producers, with a general expansion in trade and active markets.

In 1913 the Convention was put to the test for the first time. Early in that year consumption fell appreciably, production (inevitably, viewed with the benefit of hindsight) was reduced too late and stocks began to pile up. From £26 5s 0d in January the London price fell to £20 5s 0d in June 1913. When they were finally agreed and imposed, the restrictions on output were but reluctantly accepted by members of the Convention. Even had it not in fact been abandoned on the outbreak of war in August 1914, its future must already have been in doubt.

The Lead Smelters' Association was also set up in 1909, but followed a different pattern from that of the zinc cartel. In this instance, Metallgesellschaft were the prime movers, themselves controllers directly or indirectly of most of the German and other non-USA lead output. The company secured the co-operation of the major Belgian and Spanish producers in agreeing that the entire output of the cartel be marketed by Metallgesellschaft. This, therefore, was an operation along price-control rather than production-control lines, since Metallgesellschaft reckoned they would be able to sell metal to, or hold it back from, the market in such a fashion as to preclude any undue fluctuations in price.

The weak American selling that had so bedevilled the zinc convention when prices generally were falling was more or less neutralised by the terms of an agreement with the American Smelting and Refining Company (Asarco). The only apparent danger therefore would have been stocks already independently held in Europe. In the event these stocks were largely eliminated over a period, independent producers gave no trouble and the average London price of good soft pig lead rose from £12 8s 0d in 1910 to £18 15s 0d in 1913. The Association was still enjoying its rosy first years when it, too, was closed down at the outbreak of war in 1914. What it might have achieved in the longer term (and in a less generally favourable market) must therefore remain a matter for conjecture.

The First World War
The events which affected the LME both during and immediately after the First World War need to be considered in rather more detail in the context of lead and zinc than in that of the other metals. Germany represented a force of very considerable strength and influence where lead and zinc were concerned, and the way in which this situation developed during and after hostilities has a bearing on the post-war LME which should not be overlooked.

The first reaction to the inevitability of war with Germany was the closure of the LME altogether, and this took place on 31 July 1914. The motivation apears to have been more a concern over possible disruption of supplies – Germany herself was after all the main adversary – and the fear of more general shortages owing to disruption of shipping than any policy decision as to replacement of the metal trade by British Government purchasing agencies. The LME remained closed for some three months, and was re-opened on 18 November 1914 after a brief spell of unofficial trading between members; dealings at first were rather strictly confined. Lead and zinc imports from Germany and German-occupied or controlled countries naturally ceased almost at once.

Whilst the position as to lead was not critical, that of supplies of zinc to Britain was difficult in the extreme. The UK smelting industry was not large – being able to meet only about a third of domestic requirements – and the country had come to rely very heavily on German and Belgian imports. There were by this time considerable supplies of ores and concentrates available in Australia which previously had for the most part been exported to Germany for smelting. Even after the German contracts were terminated, therefore, the problem of ensuring adequate smelter capacity remained acute. By the end of 1915 zinc prices stood at three times their immediately pre-war levels, and it is thought probable that quite large speculative positions had been built up.

In consequence of these and other happenings, the British Government intervened to prevent "speculative" dealings, with the inevitable result that hedging and forward trading (other than purely physical) virtually ceased. In December 1916 complete Government control was instituted and all trading in copper, lead and zinc was suspended. What at its outset had been assumed to be a brief war was now proving almost totally disruptive as it dragged on. The effect was to eliminate from the international scene more than half of the zinc smelting capacity which had been so heavily concentrated in Germany, Belgium and France.

This situation was the cause of a major shift in the balance of zinc production; the American smelting capacity was all but doubled by 1917, and for the first time the United States exported metal both to Britain and to France. In the previous year the UK Government had contracted to buy the bulk of the Australian ore over a 10-year period. Up until then, this had been going chiefly to the German smelters for refining and with the closure of this outlet the stocks had been building up in Australia since the outbreak of war. British smelting capacity started to expand as a result, and the foundations of Australia's own electrolytic smelting industry were laid with the establishment of a plant in Tasmania.

The position with lead, though less acute, was a roughly parallel one. German control of the Spanish mines was diluted and her own very large smelting industry deprived at the same time of much of its imported ore. Again, United States capacity was increased to fill the partial vacuum left by this situation and by the fact that Mexican production had been brought to a standstill by a revolution in that country. However, the greatest expansion of lead smelting capacity took place in Australia while Canadian production was also stepped up. Both these countries remained as producers of refined lead on a world scale. The war thus both demonstrated the extent of the German control over lead and zinc production and at the same time largely dissipated that control. At the centre of the network which owned, controlled or were virtually the only buyers of ores and concentrates in widely scattered areas stood Metallgesellschaft. Along with various banking interests this company was also a co-owner of Henry R. Merton in London, which in turn controlled the Merton Metallurgical Company. Merton Metallurgical had a smelting plant in South Wales as well as interests in the United States and Australia. As the sole selling agent for these and other members of the Lead Association, Metallgesellschaft was thus in control of a large part of the world output of lead up to the First World War.

The organisation – disrespectfully styled "the Octopus" – found itself progressively sundered as the war went on. Overseas subsidiaries, for example, were re-formed so as to retain control within their countries of domicile. After the armistice the United Kingdom Government was faced with the need to reorganise the 10-year purchasing agreement with the Australian producers on a commercial basis. For this reason, the British Metal Corporation was established in November 1918 with backing from London and from Australia. This corporation's role was expanded from its original one as a purchaser of Australian zinc to that of a developer of metal production throughout the Empire.

By its very existence, BMC did cause a measure of anxiety amongst the traders in London, and fears were expressed of a monopolistic distortion of the established pattern of marketing there, either by curbing the ability of the "independents" to buy from overseas, or by direct dealings producer to consumer. In the event these fears proved quite groundless. BMC has in fact been a Ring member of the LME for very many years, although its original nomenclature has been lost in mergers and reorganisations over the passage of time. (Sir Cecil Budd was Chairman of the Board of the Metal Market & Exchange Company at the same time as he served as first Chairman of the new BMC.)

The lead and zinc markets between the wars

One curious effect of the transformation wrought on the lead and zinc markets by the war was that, for the first time, dealings in these metals took place in the main Ring in January 1920. The hegemony which had existed pre-war had been swept away, and trading on the open market now took on a significance which it had not hitherto possessed – and this no doubt to the benefit of all, including those who had previously controlled a rather stultified market.

At first, prices of all metals fell in sympathy with declining armament orders; however, it was not long before something of a boom occurred, with buying orders taking prices to historic high points. In February 1920 lead reached a price of £52 7s 6d and zinc £62 10s 0d; but reaction swiftly set in and in a year's time the prices had relapsed to £25 5s 0d and £23 10s 0d respectively. This reaction was the symptom of an overall recession in trade, which caused a situation of over-supply in all markets and notably in lead and zinc. In addition, the economic climate took a marked turn for the worse: a situation which began with the collapse of the Mark, and did not really end until after the Great Depression of 1929 to 1931. Demand in certain quarters – notably in the stripling automobile industry – did, however, give rise to some pressure on supplies. Improved methods of extraction of zinc from lead–zinc ores and increasing supplies of recycled lead (much of it recovered from old car batteries) in their turn increased the supply of these metals with the result that the general trend of prices continued downwards.

The decline in all prices began to be noticeable in the mid 1920s. One effect of the war had been greatly to increase productive capacity, with the coming on stream of modern and comparatively low-cost operations set up in Australia, Canada and elsewhere. Meantime the older-established European industry had perforce to continue to rely on less up-to-date plant, and to pay more for imported ores. Some sort of collective initiative by the European producers was felt necessary; perhaps with happy memories of the short-lived yet apparently successful Spelter Convention before the war, they formed the Zinc Cartel in May 1928.

At first the cartel was not an unqualified success. It was not until January of the following year that any form of agreement was reached as to policy; and even this agreement was far from wholehearted. There were some very basic differences in outlook between the members. Belgium and Poland, who were mainly concerned with exports, pressed for production controls, whilst

83

with an eye to their largely domestic markets Britain, France and Germany preferred some form of protective measures. The cartel also failed to attract the new (and expanding) producers of electrolytic zinc which had been set up, outside the traditional refining areas, in Australia, Canada and Mexico. These producers maintained the level of their exports to Europe and – electro zinc being of a higher and more consistent standard – made appreciable inroads on the market there. Prices, therefore, continued their downward trend and the cartel was abandoned at the end of 1929. There was talk of its revival, but no positive steps were taken. In 1931 the zinc price in London fell to an obviously uneconomic level – as low as £9 13s 9d – and it became clear to the producers that a further major co-operative effort on their part was essential if they were to protect their margins at all.

The International Zinc Cartel, formed in July 1931, was the outcome: this time all the main producers outside the USA became members. An overall reduction of output to 55% of agreed capacity was almost immediately accepted and implemented. By this means, production for the rest of the year, and 1932, was so reduced as to fall below world consumption, stocks declined correspondingly and prices took an upward turn at last.

Unfortunately for those concerned, other and very powerful disruptive influences made real co-operation between members of the cartel difficult if not actually impossible. Britain (the largest zinc importer) left the Gold Standard in September 1931. The ensuing depreciation of sterling and those currencies (e.g. the Australian pound) which moved with sterling brought a rise in the London (sterling) price which was greatly to their benefit, at the expense of producers whose currencies remained on gold. These countries were compelled to adopt protective measures in order to maintain their foreign exchange positions in the face of declining exports: amongst them were Belgium, France, Germany and Holland. To complete what was by now almost a scene of financial anarchy (with moratoria on most war debt payments already declared) the United States herself left the Gold Standard in April 1933.

Tariffs and quotas

It is small wonder, therefore, that in this climate, even traditionally free-trading countries such as the United Kingdom should have been led to seek protection for their own interests. The Import Duties Act was passed in 1932. This put an end to completely free trading with the imposition of import duties on a selective basis. In the same year the Ottawa Conference instituted the system of "Empire Preference" which was to last, as far as lead and zinc duties were concerned, right up to the British accession to the Treaty of Rome. Other colonial powers took roughly comparable steps in their own interest, these taking the form of import restrictions or (in the case of Germany) export subsidies. The Ottawa Conference led the British Government to impose a duty of 10% *ad valorem* on all imports of zinc other than from Empire sources. By 1933 Australia, Canada and Rhodesia between them contributed some 80% of British imports, compared with 34% in 1930. Imports from these sources would have been greater still, had it not been for the quota restrictions imposed by the cartel, which was still in being. In 1933 the Germans introduced a system of premiums to domestic producers. These various unilateral steps by some of its members naturally strained the cartel, and there were demands for a revision of the quotas which had been observed only somewhat approximately in any case by the low-cost producers. This brought about the suspension of the cartel in January 1933, though it was renewed in March with what were hoped to be more compelling provisions for observation of the quota limits. These were increased over the ensuing two years as world consumption recovered, but the attraction of national rather than co-operative market protection proved too strong and the cartel was finally dissolved at the end of 1934.

The Lead Producers' Reporting Association was founded in April 1931 by the majority of the non-American producers. The reasons behind the formation of the association were similar to those which had brought the zinc cartels into being. Lead had been in over-production effectively since 1925, and stocks of surplus material had amassed to an alarming degree. The London price declined inexorably until at the end of 1930 it had reached a low of £14 12s 6d per ton. The association sought to remedy the situation by restrictions on output as well as by financing stocks. For a time the price was indeed steadied, but the devaluation of sterling after Britain went off the Gold Standard in 1931, and the imposition of import duties by Britain the following year, proved too much for the association to deal with and it was dissolved in March 1932. Prices fell once more (to £9 3s 9d in June 1932), although lead from Empire sources was attracted to London even at these levels. Meanwhile, Belgium and Germany took action to protect their home industries, leaving

85

the United States, Spain and Mexico to bear the worst effects of the depression. Producers in these latter countries were quick to seize on any apparent stimulation of consumer demand and to flood a not too receptive market with their own output. In 1934 silver prices rose, leading to a further increase in lead output in order to extract the now more valuable silver content. As with other strategic commodities it was not in fact until international tension began to mount – especially on the Italian "adventure" in Abyssinia – that demand began really to recover. In fact, by March 1937 the London price of lead had strengthened to £36 7s 6d, although this price was not sustained and there was a falling-off in the months following.

The Lead Producers' Association was brought into being in September 1938, having this time strong support from all leading producers outside the United States and Europe. The association worked on the basis of production limitations linked with price movements on the LME and changes in the tonnage in stock. Thus restrictions initially were to be imposed if stocks rose to 150,000 tons or more, or the LME price fell below £15 0s 0d. Like the pre-war cartels, this association did little (or was required to do little) before its dissolution on the outbreak of the Second World War.

The LME contracts between the wars

Both the good soft pig lead and virgin spelter contracts survived unaltered for many years after their introduction. This comparative longevity was not, however, achieved without a great deal of discussion and intermittent disagreement. The conflicting requirements of a contract broad enough in scope both to satisfy producers and to serve as a useful medium for hedging, and those of consumers who would have preferred something far more precise, were always apparent. To these had to be added the complications of shipping practices (and timetables) to which the lead and zinc contracts were particularly subject. In 1923 (20 years after the introduction of the lead contract) there were strong arguments in favour of admitting Liverpool as an additional delivery point to London. Canadian and Mexican metal usually came to the United Kingdom via Liverpool and it was urged that registration of that port would facilitate the delivery of this metal on to the market. The Committee, however, felt otherwise, bearing in mind that London was then handling more than 70% of imported lead, and seeking also not to upset the important European trade which naturally made use of London rather than Liverpool. (In point of fact, London remained the only delivery point for LME lead until 1932.) The virgin spelter contract was amended to admit deliveries FOR Avonmouth in 1930, in order to accommodate the needs of the UK zinc smelting industry, itself largely a creation of the war years.

In terms of standardisation of metal deliverable against either contract there had been nothing at all laid down. Lead deliveries were reasonably consistent and complaints from consumers were few. Zinc was a different matter, however, especially since the evolution of the distillation process. Complaints were heard quite frequently and the Committee's first reaction was to exhort producers to endeavour to maintain a higher and less variable standard. However, the zinc contract was losing ground owing to the increased production of electrolytic zinc assaying 99.9% and better. In common with lead, the zinc contract as it then stood laid down no terms as to deliverable brands or purity but was based upon ex-government stocks with which the market had been re-started at the end of the First World War; and there were good ordinary brands assaying 98% Zn. As the higher grades were at the time in a position to command a premium over good ordinary brands (this was not always to be the case), they tended to be traded outside the LME contracts.

A further, and in a sense even knottier, problem was possibly the introduction of the import duties in 1932. The duties were at the outset opposed by the LME on the two grounds that they would penalise British consumers, and that they would be detrimental to the Exchange's position as arbiter of world prices and as the world's ultimate "physical market of last resort". (Indeed, the latter was the prime reason for the maintenance of a duty-free world price at all.) The contracts were re-worded to include "United Kingdom import duty (if any) to be for buyer's account", and provision was made for a claw-back of duty in the event that foreign material was re-exported and not consumed within the United Kingdom. The trouble here was that metal imported from Empire sources came rapidly to command a premium equivalent to the duty imposed on foreign imports, were it sold privately outside the market. Consequently, this material practically disappeared from market trading, turnover fell accordingly, and LME prices came to be based to an excessive extent on dealings in foreign material which all too often was only offered there *faute de mieux*.

The situation was thus unhealthy for the market and for producers alike: the one saw turnover diminishing and the other saw prices (often needlessly low) based more and more on sales of production other than their own. The Committee of the LME and the Import Duties Advisory Committee of the UK Government held discussions in August 1935. As a consequence, specific duties were imposed in lieu of the controversial *ad valorem* duties. These amounted to a flat 7s 6d per ton on lead and 12s 6d on zinc imported from other than Empire sources. The LME contracts were also amended, to permit the seller either to deliver foreign metal at contract price with duty added, or domestic or Empire metal with an added premium equal to the amount of the duty. In either case the impost was for the buyer's account.

In this way, both Empire and foreign lead and zinc were traded in the market on precisely the same basis as to price. What is equally important was that the impossibility of hedging an *ad valorem* duty on an as yet unknown price was also resolved. (As an historical note, the duty on zinc was raised to 30s per ton in 1939.)

The Second World War
The outbreak of the Second World War once again saw all dealings on the LME in copper, lead and zinc suspended. Private stocks in the UK were requisitioned, and the new Ministry of Supply fixed maximum official prices for each. It was unfortunate that the Committee of the Exchange were not consulted beforehand, for these arbitrary prices were well below current market prices. (It is arguable that these latter may at the time have been a little over-high, in the light of immediately pre-war market sentiment.) Be that as it may, the closing-out of open positions was not achieved without difficulty and even a measure of acrimony. The Ministry was also – to market eyes at least – dilatory in releasing metal for completion of delivery contracts, no doubt on account of natural disinclination to part with strategic materials. In the event, lead and zinc deliveries were not completed until the end of February 1940.

The LME thus passed into a kind of limbo (tin dealings were suspended, and the Ring ceased to trade, on 8 December 1941 after the Japanese entry into the conflict threatened supplies from the East), and was to remain so until 1944. Not that Board or Committee were idle: the Rules were revised and a good deal of useful propaganda work was undertaken. In 1944 discussions with the authorities were initiated with a view to a recommencement of free trading. Lead and zinc at this time were actually in surplus along with copper, only tin being scarce.

In May 1945 the British Government terminated its long-term contracts with producers of lead and zinc, licences for domestic consumption became more readily available and imports actually reduced for a time as accumulated stocks were pressed into service. Government policy was still undecided, however, and was no doubt rendered doubly cautious in the light of the serious disruption of, and actual damage to, sources of supply which the war had occasioned. In point of fact it was not for some three or four years after the cessation of hostilities that supply positions could be regarded as in any way restored.

However, the demand situation was causing concern; the United States appeared as a consumer of heroic proportions (60% of the free world's copper and 40% or so of lead and zinc), and in consequence emerged for the first time as an importer. Coupled with the desire on the part of most other countries to acquire US dollars, this new trend put a considerable impetus into rising prices for all metals.

As an indication of price movements, lead had been pegged at £25 per ton throughout the war. It rose to £55 by July 1946 and to £90 by May 1947. The bulk-buying policy of the Government was too inflexible, the Ministry's requirements too large for them to be other than a focus of attention whenever it came into the world market. Worse still, when the inevitable downward trend started in early 1949 the Ministry lowered its own selling prices to UK consumers far too cautiously and clumsily. The outcome was that in May of that year the London price of zinc was £24 per ton dearer than in New York, and the lead price £18 dearer.

For a brief period, the Ministry attempted to follow New York prices, and a very limited form of hedging was permitted to British consumers in that they could book forward orders (on payment of a premium) as a form of cover against rising prices. There was no comparable cover for merchants or holders of stocks against falls in prices, however. This well-intentioned half-measure on the one hand, and a real concern as to use of metals in "commodity shunting" operations involving further exchange losses on the other, were enough to stay the Government's hand until the re-opening of the tin market – tin being a sterling commodity – in November 1949.

Conditions generally became far less easy after that date, and it is of interest to note that – still controlled and dealt with entirely by the Ministry of Materials, as it was now styled – prices for lead rose to £180 per ton and zinc to £190 in August 1951. Even higher prices were obtaining on the black market: £240 for zinc and £200 for lead at the time. The Ministry was once again caught with long-term buying orders at high prices when the market declined once more after the end of the Korean War. Once again recourse was made to following New York prices, but despite fairly savage cuts (£60 per ton in May and June 1952) the London prices remained uneconomically high in relation to those in New York and on the Continent.

The markets re-opened

Clearly the situation could not be allowed to continue. After further hesitation the Government (now a Conservative one) announced that dealings in lead would be freed as from 1 October 1952. At the same time, Government purchasing and the issue of licences were done away with, and the Bank of England scheme (initiated with the re-opening of dealings in tin) was extended to cover the foreign exchange aspect of lead dealings. Cash lead was made available, and the Ministry was also a lender of lead – through the "Government Broker" – until private supplies were restored.

Resumption in dealings brought at first a heavy fall in prices. The Ministry's last selling price had been £131 per ton; this was known to be unrealistic since it was still based on the New York price, which was derived from a very narrow and somewhat isolated market. The European "going price" was £95. In the event the LME price after 3 weeks of free trading stood at £80. There was soon a recovery as consumers started seriously to buy, yet the producers at the time were not very pleased with the immediate outcome of the return to free trading after some years of insulation from market forces.

The zinc market on the LME was re-opened on 2 January 1953. There had been a little more caution in this case, as it had to be taken into account that some 50% of UK imports of zinc came at the time from Canada and the United States. A drain in dollar reserves could therefore have ensued. As against this, experience with tin and lead had shown that a fall in prices was to be expected – so reducing the strain on the country's exchange position. The latter forecast proved correct, with prices rapidly falling from the Ministry's £110 right down to £63 10s 0d by the end of April.

With the freeing of dealings in copper on 5 August 1953 the LME was once more fully operational – after an eclipse lasting 14 years.

At this point, it is only right to mention the name of Mr J. D. ("Jimmy") Wolff, who came to the market as an Authorised Clerk in 1904, chaired the Committee for a remarkable span from 1928 until 1950 save for one year, and the Board from 1946 to 1961. He was largely responsible for all the re-negotiations with Ministers during the war years and those immediately following, in which he was well supported by P. W. Smith, the uncle of the redoubtable Philip Smith, who is the present Chairman of the Board. Smith and Wolff are names which can trace an uninterrupted connection with the Exchange from its foundation to the present time, and the combination of P. G. Smith and Freddy Wolff as Chairmen of Board and Committee respectively was one under which the author was happy to serve for almost the whole of his time at the LME.

A world surplus of lead developed during the 1950s. In consequence of this, and of the imposition of protective measures by some of the producing countries (in December 1957 the LME price had sunk to £70), the United Nations set up the Lead and Zinc Conference in 1959. Prices continued to fall, lead being at £61 17s 6d in December 1960, and a year later falling to £57 12s 6d. The conference was developed into the Lead–Zinc Study Group, whose members meet each year at a conference in Geneva.

The lead price did show a recovery as far as £154 10s 0d late in 1964, but fell away once more as over-supply combined with concern as to lead pollutant effects (especially as an additive in motor fuel) down to a low of £84 in late 1972. There was a recovery in the boom of 1973 to 1974, whereafter the price again fell away, despite the efforts of producers to support it by buying on the LME.

Zinc prices were sustained in the 1950s by growing demand, and by stockpiling in the USA, to peak at £96 17s 6d in December 1959. After two years of uncertainty, during which a low of £62 was recorded in August 1962, zinc prices advanced once more to reach £148 10s 0d in July 1964. This rapid advance brought a measure of concern as to substitution (plastics for galvanised products, for example), and on 13 July 1964 the Imperial Smelting Company issued a statement to the effect that, as stocks of zinc in LME warehouses were reduced to a "negligible tonnage", the producers supplying the UK and Continental markets considered LME prices no longer realistic. The Imperial Smelting Company therefore decided to give the lead by introducing their own price of £125 per ton. "This price", the statement read, "is effective today and will remain in force until further notice."

The LME price fell shortly afterwards, and the Imperial Smelting Company's – or European producer – price was lowered to £110. In May the following year the LME price dipped below the European producer price again, and the producers revised their prices downwards to £102 and in June 1967 to £98. This was then raised once more to £114 6s 8d after Britain's devaluation in November. Thereafter the LME price and the producer price moved in a narrow band: usually in sympathy, usually with the LME standing at a discount roughly equal to the cost of duty and shipment from the Continent to the United Kingdom. The European zinc producers' system makes use of a "fixed" price which varies from time to time on the more frequent variations in the LME price. At the same time, the producers can and do move to support LME prices by themselves operating on the market. The success or otherwise of the system is somewhat clouded by the fact that the LME contract remains 98% Zn (good ordinary brand – GOB) while much of the material in use is of higher purity with consequential premiums over the LME prices. There have been times, however, when the market has been further confused by shortages of good ordinary brand – whose lead content makes it a requirement of the galvanising trade – and surplus of high-grade or special high-grade. Perhaps things will not really be satisfactory until the LME introduces a high-grade zinc contract as has already been done in the case of tin.

The lead and zinc contracts after the Second World War

The original GSP lead and virgin spelter contracts enjoyed a remarkably long span of life. It was not until after the war that changes were made which brought them more on a par with the current contracts for copper and tin. On the re-opening of the Exchange for dealings in lead and zinc, the contracts were changed in order to limit deliverable material to any one of a number of approved brands: a measure, this, of protection to the consumer.

It was not until July 1960 that, as with lead, the delivery terms in the zinc contract were amended from ex-ship to in-warehouse for prompts maturing after 1 October; the warehouse warrant thus became for these two metals, also, the basic document traded in respect of LME dealings. (The changeover resulted in an immediate increase of about £1 in prices.) This alteration was effected only after much discussion between Board and Committee culminating in a General Meeting of Subscribers held in March 1960.

In 1966 Rotterdam was added to the delivery points for lead and zinc. This greatly altered the pattern of trading, since the Rotterdam warehouses were in a position to store metal without payment of duty or premium unless or until that material was taken into use within the European Economic Community or (if dutiable) within the United Kingdom. Further complications arose, to the extent that in later years stocks of Korean zinc in Rotterdam reached large proportions owing to complications over import quotas of Eastern Bloc metal permitted to enter the Community. For a time it appeared as though the LME were destined to be a home for this "homeless" metal, until changing conditions in 1973–74 drastically reduced stocks and altered the whole picture. (The Committee had in fact approved Hamburg as a delivery point for lead and zinc in December 1973.)

Discussion continues to take place from time to time as to the desirability of making changes in the zinc contract. It is true that in some ways it is not a wholly, or perhaps not a continually, successful one.

As it stood, the contract specified good delivery to be metal assaying not less than 98% Zn, thus leaving 2% for impurities – quite a large margin. It is the nature of these impurities that can cause serious problems for consumers buying zinc on the LME for physical delivery and not merely for long-hedging purposes. For certain end-users a high proportion of lead in the "spare" 2% is not only acceptable but desirable: these purposes include, for example, hot-dip galvanising of steel sheet for use in areas exposed to corrosion by weather. Other users of zinc, notably alloyers, abhor the presence of lead and would in any event prefer a higher zinc content. It is really a matter of such widely differing end-uses as to produce two quite different types of metal. Two contracts, then? At first sight this appears to be the simple and logical answer. This course, if taken, could well give rise to two further problems. The first of these would be doubt as to the viability of two zinc contracts, whose existence stemmed from the divergence of consumer requirements only, and took no account of the total volume of zinc business passing through the LME. Greater opportunities would have been afforded for those seeking physical offtake from the market, but we know already that – even on the LME – physical deliveries are but a small fraction of total turnover. The risk would be to split one imperfect yet viable contract into two, neither of which would attract sufficient interest to sustain an active market and in so doing to signal a true world price. This is still the imponderable hanging over the tin market after the introduction of a second contract.

The second consequence would, of course, be that of – perhaps needlessly – interfering with a contract which, whatever its shortcomings from the consumer's point of view as to physical trading, does afford an adequate vehicle for hedging purposes. As to pricing, it may well be better to have left things as they are and to accept the fact of an off-market premium in certain instances for high-grade or special high-grade zinc. Not that it is always so. There was a period in 1973 when a shortage of GOB 98% zinc led for a while to a wide backwardation and to premiums for this humble grade over others of higher purity. Rumour at the time had it, indeed, that users of GOB for galvanising purposes were perforce taking in high-grade and debasing it with lead in order to arrive at the equivalent of GOB!

The lead contract has not suffered in this way, and the recurring problem with this market on the LME is the spasmodic series of invasions by speculators of what is by tradition very much a traders' market. The attraction of LME lead in this context is that whilst it is an industrial metal like copper, and therefore one whose likely movements in price may be predicted in roughly the same manner, it costs as a rule something like half as much to speculate in lead as it does in copper. These speculative forays, however, are neither so frequent nor in general so disturbing as to constitute any real threat to the authority of the contract in its chief role, i.e. that of an indicator of world prices for the metal.

Neither of these two contracts is perfect, though that for zinc poses less tractable problems, and neither has the glamour of copper or the seductive appeal of tin to the would-be manipulator; yet each has a respectable history within that of the LME itself and each has its place in the overall metal trading scene.

8
Aluminium and Nickel

Though these two metals appear to have little enough in common, the contracts may be considered together as being the first totally new contracts introduced on the LME during the years following the Second World War. Since the end of the war, many outside factors both economic and political had combined to produce a climate very different from the *laissez-faire* atmosphere which prevailed at least for a good deal of the time in which earlier contracts had been launched.

Another point of similarity between the two is that, in each case, the LME has succeeded in bringing in a contract in a metal whose supply – and whose pricing structure – had by tradition been very much the preserve of powerful and well-organised producer groups.

Aluminium

The processes which go towards the production of aluminium are very different from those behind that of other non-ferrous metals. With these, the procedure is basically that of mining or dredging ore, processing it so as to remove the bulk of the impurities and arrive at concentrates, and then refining these by furnace smelting or in some cases (such as copper cathode) by electrolysis or distillation. Aluminium is different.

Though it is the most abundant of the metals, aluminium's basic "raw material", bauxite, contains aluminium only in a highly contaminated form and one which demands heavy (some would say profligate) expenditure of energy in the refining process. This energy

THE LONDON METAL EXCHANGE

requirement, and the efficiency of hydro-electric power in meeting it, has led to the establishment of important producers of aluminium in Canada, Norway and Switzerland. Perhaps for this reason – very high capital outlay and running expenses in the smelter restricting their numbers – the aluminium producers have developed in a manner which gives the whole industry a vertically integrated form. Thus, from the mining and the intake of bauxite, fluorspar and other ingredients of the alumina from which the metal is refined, down through smelting and on to marketing fabricated shapes, the entire chain of operations tends to be if not literally under one roof then more often than not figuratively in one pair of hands.

It is axiomatic in the world of commodity markets that producers view the free market with, to say the least, a measure of caution. Producers who are in a strongly entrenched position and who are relatively few in number though very large in substance sometimes carry through this cautious attitude to one of suspicion verging upon downright hostility. It is not our purpose here to analyse this attitude, for which it may be confessed there is on occasion a mite of justification. But we should take note of it when viewing the somewhat protracted efforts on the part of the LME to mount an aluminium contract in the face of it.

The increasing use of aluminium in a wide variety of applications soon made it attractive as a potential LME metal. Price movements were usually in large and quite unpredictable steps as the producers in concert moved the prices up and down; this, after the end of the war, was already making merchants and consumers think seriously of the desirabiity of being able to hedge, as well as to see a price made daily in open market. The metal was by then widely used in the airframe industry, where before the more recent crop of mergers there was an abundance of small to medium-sized companies all vying for a share of a highly competitive market; the same could be said of suppliers to the construction industry. Aluminium was coming increasingly into use in general engineering also, its relative freedom from corrosion, light weight and extreme malleability making it attractive for castings either by itself or as a constituent in an alloy such as mazak, of which many automobile engine components are made.

But perhaps most significantly in our context here, the metal was beginning to make inroads into territory hitherto held almost exclusively by copper in the electrical field. Though its conductivity is not as great as that of copper – roughly one and a half times the mass of aluminium is required – its highly competitive price was making it increasingly attractive for bus-bars and for the larger cables where compactness was not at a premium. This has in fact brought about the introduction of cupronal, an aluminium bus-bar overlaid with a thin coating of copper.

As we have seen, it was largely on account of concern over this price competition by aluminium in electrical applications which led the copper producers into their exercise in holding down prices in the early 1960s.

There had been discussion on the topic of an aluminium contract on the LME as long ago as 1958, but it would appear that this went no further than discussion and a certain amount of market research of a not very intense nature. Certainly nothing more positive occurred until 1971, when the subject was raised once more (along with that of nickel, as it happened) and a sub-committee was formed to explore the possibilities for a contract. One of the first actions taken, curiously enough, was the despatch of letters to the major aluminium producers canvassing their views on the matter. Those who replied did so in no uncertain terms: true to tradition the producers were hostile. Unperturbed, the sub-committee went ahead with the preparation of a contract and with drafting a sub-mission to the Bank of England propounding the benefits afforded by a market where prices are openly made and where hedging becomes a real aid to producer and consumer alike. (At that time the Bank exercised a watchdog function where commodity markets were concerned, in the course of its duties in the enforcement of exchange control regulations. As a bonus, this put the Bank and its senior officials into a position of being – though in no official way – an excellent link between the markets and Whitehall.) During the early months of 1972 other events affecting the LME and its members had the effect of relegating the aluminium study to the background, and it was allowed to lapse for some five further years.

It should be added here that during this period the LME did receive many expressions of support for a free market in aluminium from merchants and consumers, especially those on the Continent of Europe. This support was later to stand the Aluminium Sub-committee in good stead.

The merchants and consumers within the EEC were facing a difficult situation, in that in keeping with its protectionist outlook the EEC Commission had imposed a duty of no less than 7.5% *ad*

97

valorem on aluminium imported into the Community. (In fairness, it should also be noted that the Directorate-General concerned with competition – roughly akin to the UK's Office of Fair Trading – was also looking askance at the cartel-like appearance of the producing side of the industry.) This duty was in the main directed against metal coming into the Community from Eastern Bloc countries – as was the case with the import restrictions on Comecon zinc – where Romania in particular was an active producer and would-be exporter. In their turn, the Romanians were in favour of an LME contract, and sent a deputation to London for discussions with the sub-committee. They would have been willing to stock the new market with their own product in order to ensure adequate "chips" for a liquid market from the outset. However, this welcome affability had perforce to be treated with a little caution, since not only could there have been problems with too many of the initial stocks attributable to the market subject to the *ad valorem* duty, but there was also the matter of the purity of the metal proffered and the nature of its impurities. This is rather critical in the case of aluminium.

The last, and ultimately successful, progression towards an aluminium contract commenced in 1977, again with the setting-up of a sub-committee – under M. L. Connor, the same Chairman as in 1971. This time, the ground was more exhaustively covered and one happy step was the setting-up of a working party which included experts from outside the Committee and indeed from outside the LME itself. (This is a step quite often taken by other markets in exploring new contracts – for example in the setting-up of what is now the International Petroleum Exchange of London – but not, it would appear, previously taken by the LME.)

With the expert advice of members of the working party, a case was rapidly put together for the establishment of an aluminium contract on the LME. In it, the shortcomings of the cartel or quasi-cartel method of setting prices was demonstrated to the extent, as was plain later on, of severely upsetting some of the major producers who lost no time in putting their own case for maintaining the *status quo*. In this context, one well remembers some fairly tense meetings in the office of the Department of Trade when representatives of the LME and of the producers faced each other across the table – all men who knew and respected each other but whose views were at variance over this one issue.

A further factor militating in favour of an LME contract was the greatly changing climate in the world of international metal marketing. New and independent smelters were being put into commission or being planned in areas outside the traditional ones, and the merchant trade in Europe had grown enormously, with considerable stocks being held – and in need of hedging.

The basic terms of the proposed contract were to be similar to those for copper: warrants of 25 tonnes (the 1000 kilo or 2204 lb unit was now standard) with a three-month forward period and a minimum fluctuation of 50p.

However, differences began to emerge when the special rules governing specification and so forth were being settled by the working party. It had been decided at an early stage that, initially at any rate, the contract would apply only to virgin aluminium and that secondary, or recycled, metal would not be a good delivery. As to shape, ingot was decided upon out of something of a plethora of differing shapes, mostly arrived at by extrusion at the smelter itself as distinct from the separate activities of the fabricator in other metals. Recently, T-bar has been added as a deliverable shape.

The major matters discussed were those pertaining to purity. Here, there are two significant differences between the aluminium and the other LME contracts. Though the purity requirement was set fairly high, at 99.50% Al (after debate as to other standards which were also widely used by consumers), it was decided to limit by definition the percentage of certain intruders known to occur in the metal. Thus, the contract specifies that the metal be not less than 99.50% Al and furthermore that it shall contain no more than 0.40% iron and 0.30% silicon. It is interesting to think of this specific exclusion, or limiting, of named impurities in the context of the GOB zinc contract.

Further to ensure the quality, and concomitant lack of unwelcome impurities in deliverable aluminium, steps were taken to lay down firm rules as to the first placing of metal on warrant to take its place in the tonnage being traded, or eligible to be traded, on the LME. To this end a whole new clause has been written into the Special Rules section of the contract. A producer's certificate of analysis must accompany the metal and this must confirm the purity and state the "heat number". (This latter refers to the smelting batch of which the parcel of metal forms a part.) Should the producer's certificate not be forthcoming, an analysis must be made by an LME-approved assayer.

A certificate of origin must also accompany the parcel, this being required by reason of the EEC duty on imported metal, of which we have already taken note.

To prevent the foregoing requirements putting an unacceptable burden of responsibility on the warehouseman, each delivery for placing on warrant for the first time must be sponsored by a Ring member, who assumes responsibility for documentation as to the quality. In this requirement, the contract is comparable with that on the Gold Futures Market.

Trading in aluminium on the LME was initiated in October 1978, some 20 years after those earlier recorded moves in that direction. From the outset the contract showed itself workable, and to have met the needs of the trade generally. As is so often the case with such an innovation, familiarity with it has diminished producer opposition to the point of at least tacit support.

Nickel

As with aluminium, nickel, too, had attracted the attention of the Committee some time before the contract was actually brought into being. A Nickel Sub-committee had been set up in late 1970 to explore the possibilities, and a certain amount of market research was undertaken. However, the almost total dominance of the nickel market by one major producer, whose posted price was to all intents and purposes the world price, made the project an impossibly difficult one. A further factor militating against the likely success of an LME contract was the dearth of a viable merchant market.

With time, and with shifting economic fortunes, this producer dominance of the market was eroded sufficiently for the matter to be brought up once more, and a fresh attempt was made with a re-formed sub-committee in the autumn of 1978. Once again, a campaign of despatching letters to producers was mounted, eliciting a far less unfavourable response than had been forthcoming from the earlier aluminium campaign.

There were, however, considerable technical problems to be overcome, not least amongst which was the wide variety of shapes and forms of nickel in daily use. This was a consequence of the number of specialised uses for the metal and their demands for particular forms of it. Again, and in common with aluminium, it was decided early on that only primary metal should be deliverable under the proposed contract.

The quality to be admitted was 99.8% Ni, and only the out-turn of a limited number of producers from amongst those now competing in the market was to be acceptable.

As to shapes and sizes, here the contract is more exacting in its demands than those for the other base metals. Cathodes, pellets and briquettes were specified, and in the case of cathodes sizes were laid down ranging in three steps from 4 in. × 4 in. down to 1 in. × 1 in., with tolerances limited to "internationally accepted trade practice".

The smallness in size of the individual pieces making up a parcel posed a new problem. How might they be assembled in order to make up a warrant? For example, 25 tonnes of copper is made up from a moderate quantity of cathodes or wirebars even when the smaller of the permitted sizes are offered. Traditionally, parcels of nickel in the shapes to be deliverable under the contract are packed in sealed steel drums and this was accepted as the only practicable method for the LME also, although it does preclude any form of "snap" inspection as to the composition of a parcel on warrant.

The responsibility for ensuring that the drums were indeed full of nickel and not some less marketable substance was accepted by the warehouses. Under the nickel contract, each drum offered for placing on warrant must be opened, its contents inspected, and the drum re-sealed by the accepting warehouse. The cost of this laborious operation is borne by the party placing the metal on warrant and a named Ring member must accept responsibility for the placing. The warrants must in the first instance be issued to the order of the member sponsor. Each parcel of 6 tonnes must emanate from the same refinery and consist wholly of one of the permitted shapes and sizes. This warrant weight is yet another peculiarity of the nickel contract, which arises from the number of drums which may be stowed in a standard road or rail container.

The contract was launched not long after that for aluminium and it, too, has shown itself to be viable from the outset, and to attract an adequate supporting volume of business. Perhaps surprisingly, in such a comparatively recondite material, this business is not by any means confined to trade hedging and pricing: the nickel contract has also an appeal to some of the more expert non-trade elements.

With the coincidence in time of the introduction of the new contract and the onset of a worldwide depression, it is perhaps premature as yet to pass judgement on its performance. The auguries for a metal with a preponderance of its end-uses connected with steelmaking are, however, encouraging in the long term.

101

9

Precious and "Special" Metals

By tradition associated with the industrial metals, the LME has also extended its trading activities towards others more exotic, or with very different uses. Of these, silver should come first to our attention since trading in this metal has been established in the Ring for many years. The connection with gold is both more recent and less completely direct, but because it is none the less a very real connection, and because the technique and the form of the Gold Futures Market may well come to influence LME trading generally, it merits inclusion in these pages.

The silver market
The present silver contract on the LME is in fact the third to have been instituted in this metal. As early in the Exchange's history as 1897, dealings in silver were admitted into the Ring. This development became feasible when the bullion merchants took the step of issuing warrants in respect of metal held by them in vault, thus making it possible to trade in documents of title, themselves freely negotiable, to set quantities of metal of known description and quality. Buying and selling silver "sight unseen" was now a reality on to which could be grafted the established technique of buying and selling for future delivery and of closing-out futures positions by a countervailing transaction. This first silver contract remained in being until the commencement of the First World War, although it had actually been more or less moribund since 1911.

The second silver contract was not instituted until 1935 and like its predecessor was destined to cease trading on the outbreak of war; interest in it had not in any case been maintained at any sort of active level. After the cessation of hostilities the question of re-instituting a silver contract was discussed from time to time, but no positive steps were taken until the 1960s.

At this point, and before going on to consider the third, and to date the current, silver contract on the LME, we should pay some attention to the London Silver Market. This informal body comprising bullion dealers in London has been in existence since the 1880s. When it first opened the LSM conducted a weekly price fixing with trading between members and their clients continuing on a daily basis between the fixings, which were themselves made a once-daily affair at about the turn of the century. Both spot and forward prices are made and become the yardstick for dealings until the next fixing.

In its earlier years the LSM had been to some extent haunted by the spectre of monetary silver. The metal has in fact a longer history, in Europe at any rate, than gold as a unit of exchange; the use of silver in coin both solid and in "sandwich" form persisted until the final debasement to cupro-nickel. This direct connection between silver and money has long been eroded, almost to the point of disappearance, but the metal has been and remains an important medium for hedging changes in currency values. However, the main activities of the infant LSM were for the most part directed towards physical trading as an entrepôt market, between producers in the Americas and buyers located for the most part in China and India. Its dealings, though, were at the time subject to the vagaries of government decisions and to changes in monetary policy, since the metal still had a direct and important part to play in such matters.

The first changes in this pattern of trade occurred with the advent in 1933 of President Roosevelt's New Deal Administration in the United States. American silver prices were raised, with a consequent reversal of the flow of demand – this time from Asia back to the United States – to the extent of forcing China to abandon the Silver Standard. After about 18 months, the American Administration altered its policy to one of purchasing only domestically produced silver. A special Silver Profits Tax was also imposed on US dealers, and for the duration of this tax silver ceased to be traded on the New York Commodity Exchange. In this way, the US Treasury was able to amass very large quantities of silver into its coffers.

103

After the Second World War, the growth of the electronics industry added a new dimension to the demand for silver (already widely used in X-ray and photographic emulsions as well as in more traditional decorative guises), and in consequence demand began greatly to outstrip supply, even though the latter was sometimes augmented by releases from privately hoarded stocks. The balance of the American official stocks was released from time to time by the US Treasury at a fixed price, until in 1961 "free stocks" in the United States were exhausted. London prices – dominated by the New York price – had varied between 77*d* and 80*d* per ounce, equivalent to 89 to 92 cents. The US official selling price was raised in 1963 to 129.3 cents per ounce.

This was in fact the highest to which the price could have been raised, without the silver content of the then US coinage actually exceeding the face value of that coinage. This had the effect of putting some sort of ceiling over prices in London, too, and they remained approximately constant at around 112*d* until 18 May 1967, when US sales to foreign buyers were terminated. This move signalled an instant leap by the London price of 18½*d* to 130*d* per ounce, the largest increase since the 1949 sterling devaluation.

On 14 July 1967 the United States abandoned its attempts at maintaining a ceiling on silver prices, and sales were limited to 2 million ounces per week, to American industrial users only, and these from stocks which at the beginning of 1959 had totalled 1900 million ounces. (During the same period, the United States had abandoned silver coinage and gone over to the cupro-nickel "sandwich" coin.)

By late 1967 the American Treasury was further embarrassed by the decline in the stocks available to it of 0.999 fine bars which at the time were the accepted standard grade for the greater part of both domestic and overseas business. On 12 October that year, the US Treasury suspended sales of silver of this quality, offering instead bars of 0.996 and 0.998 fine. At the same time it was announced that these lower grades would be delivered only against "Silver Certificates", or bills first issued in 1878 and redeemable in silver. There were in fact 2127 million dollars worth of these bills in circulation at the close of 1960. In the following year any further issue was cancelled, and the old bills were called in. None the less, there were many who chose to hold them, and in 1967 there were still some 375 million or more in circulation. The last day for redemption of these Silver Certificates was fixed at 24 June 1968.

The devaluation of sterling in November 1967 brought a peak in London silver prices, and on 14 December the market there reached its high of 224¾d per ounce.

A new LME silver contract

It was hardly surprising that these developments had not been allowed to pass unnoticed by the LME. The question of re-instituting LME dealings in silver was raised in June 1967, after several members had expressed interest. Talks were held with the bullion brokers, who evinced surprise at the proposition mixed with a measure of disapprobation; but it was agreed that the discussions should be continued.

In the meantime, both the Bank of England and the Board of Trade were consulted and neither objected. The LME Committee therefore set up a sub-committee to go into the matter in detail and to draw up a contract. It soon became plain to all that this contract would have to be somewhat different from those currently in force for the other metals, notably as to the duration of the permitted forward trading period. Something longer than three months but not longer than 13 was the general consensus; but opinions varied as to precisely how long the period should be. Eventually, the sub-committee came down in favour of a seven-month period. It was felt that this would attract business from the United States and from the Continent as well as from within the United Kingdom.

The silver contract has a definite place in the history of the LME documents, in that, for the first time ever, the margin to be called from the client by the member in the event of a price movement adverse to the former was put on a mandatory as distinct from a discretionary basis. This was felt to be necessary in view of the relatively greater length of the contract and consequentially larger scope for such price movements during its course. (An argument against longer-term contracts in the other metals is that margins might then need to be mandatory, with the possibility of disturbing cash-flow considerations in hedging by industry.) Thus, a margin of 10% was laid down from the outset as essential on opening a silver contract. This could be made up by cash or a bank guarantee, and was to be maintained at 10% of the value of the contract throughout its life. Calls were to be made in steps, whenever the price difference exceeded 50% of the original margin. However, like all the LME contracts, the silver contract was set up as an agreement between principals. A side-effect of this running true to tradition was that the margin was (and is) called by the LME member himself and not via any sort of clearing house.

Contract lots were fixed at 10,000 troy ounces of silver assaying not less than 0.999 fine. There was some discussion at the time as to whether deliverable lots might comprise bars from more than one refiner, but in the event this was not permitted. Originally, storage of silver on LME warrant was confined to vaults in the Westminster Bank in London and in the AmRo Bank in Rotterdam; since then, the scope of approved delivery points has been extended.

Dealings commence

In February 1968 the new silver contract was launched on the LME. At the outset, the contract confounded the sceptics (who saw little future for two parallel silver markets in London) and the first year's turnover totalled 21,419 lots of 10,000 ounces. However, prices declined appreciably from an early peak in May of 264*d* to a low of 161*d* in June the following year: a fall of nearly 40% in direct contrast to the currently rising prices in the other metals.

It is likely that this early divergence by the silver market from the paths taken by those in the base metals arose out of an astute realisation by speculators of the virtues of the contracts as a currency hedge. Without the restrictions attached to trading in gold, and still retaining memories (if nothing more tangible) of its days as a monetary metal, silver undoubtedly possesses great attraction in this context.

In the meantime, the US silver stocks had come down from 1900 million ounces in 1959 to 110 million only by 1970 – rather less than one-quarter of annual world demand. At the time, demand world-wide was running well ahead of mine production, though the markets were "topped up" from time to time by releases from hoards as well as by a fairly consistent flow of secondary material. The sources of these replenishments were mainly India and Pakistan, in what was at the time an illicit trade via the Trucial States bordering the Persian Gulf, and from the remelting of demonetarised coin. This accumulation developed to such an extent that private holdings actually rose by nearly 220 million ounces: roughly equal to the year's sales by the US Treasury to consumers, for minting and in redemption of Silver Certificates. GSA stockpile sales were to cease in 1970, by which time it was thought that supply and demand for industrial (excluding speculative) purposes would be approximately in balance. With the speculators – and currency hedging – as the big imponderables, therefore, the LME silver market looked both highly uncertain as to prices and highly stimulating; already in early 1969 the prospects for a contract of longer duration than seven months were being canvassed. It was felt that a 12- or 13-month period would attract further business, especially from New York.

The sterling situation in 1969

LME dealings in silver had been brought within the scope of the Bank of England Metals Scheme for foreign exchange from the inception of the contract. Members, therefore, were under the same disciplines as already applied to their trade with non-residents in the other metals.

Towards the end of 1969 the UK Treasury became concerned at the increasing stocks of silver in London, whose purchase from other than British residents was felt to be putting an undue strain on the country's reserves. In December the Bank of England obtained the agreement of the bullion brokers that they would reduce the level of their silver stocks financed by UK residents – where necessary – to the levels obtaining at the beginning of that year. The Bank also communicated with the LME and meetings took place between members of the Exchange's Bank of England Liaison Committee and representatives of the Bank, in order to arrive at a *modus operandi* whereunder any surplus should not "spill over" on to the LME and so reduce the effectiveness of the restraint accepted by the bullion brokers. (In fact, LME members who dealt in silver were to be asked by the Bank to agree to a "base level" of UK-financed stocks and not to exceed that level. These base levels were to be set at figures obtaining later in the year than those accepted by the bullion brokers, and thus could be said to represent a lesser degree of restriction.)

It was also suggested that LME members might see fit or be able to finance their stocks by overseas borrowing or by "lending" silver to non-resident clients: even to the extent of using Eurodollars for the purpose.

The Committee were greatly vexed by the element of compulsion embodied in these proposals and were not shy of voicing their feelings. However, agreement to co-operate with the request was not withheld, and through the Liaison Committee regular and close contact was maintained with the Bank. Resistance from the LME was naturally based on two possibilities: first that the London market and the London price might lose their authoritativeness, and secondly that of other markets being set up as a result of London's temporary loss of freedom of action.

The Metals Scheme here came into its own. The LME had pointed out to the Bank that under the principals' contract the Exchange as such was not in a position to "police" its members' silver positions. In the event, these continued to be disclosed in confidence by participating members to the appropriate department of the Bank itself. The crisis gradually resolved itself and no coercive measures were in the end found necessary. Instead, the voluntary limitations agreed to by LME and London Silver Market members proved adequate.

A longer contract is proposed

In June 1971 the Committee again turned its attention to the possibility of a silver contract with a longer forward dealing period than seven months. A sub-committee had been looking into the matter and had come forward with the suggestion that the period be extended to 13 months – this with an eye to more business from clients in the United States as well as arbitrage with Comex in New York. Another innovation was that the margin should henceforth be discretionary (as in the other contracts) as contrasted with mandatory.

The problem was that of security against price movements in a long-duration contract without enforced margins, and an extremely ingenious solution was proposed. In brief, this was based on the continuance of "traditional" daily dealings up to three months forward, with periodic settlements of differences on a monthly basis thereafter. The settlement prices for these ensuing months would be worked out as the average of the three months sellers for the preceding five market days plus or minus the average of the difference between the three months and 13 months sellers for the same five days, divided *pro rata* for each month and rounded up to the nearest 0.1p (the minimum fluctuation in silver since decimalisation of the pound). It was of course intended that cash, three, seven and 13 months prices would be quoted each day. These settlements were to take place, as near as holidays permitted, on the fifteenth day of each month after the third month. This was in order to ensure that every position beyond three months was subject to at least one such intermediate settlement, and that the only time when anyone could have more than one month's run before an intermediate settlement would be when his position had moved into the normal three-month period.

Another point in favour of the proposed periodic settlements beyond three months, apart from that of security, was that such settlements provided only for 10 positions (dates). Were the traditional daily prompts system to have been projected so far forward, it would have produced a plethora of dates up to 13 months ahead – with consequent difficulty in quoting a meaningful price for each, in view of the uncertain volume of deals done on each of so many dates.

In sum, this was a most ingenious and worthy scheme, and one which if put into effect might well have served as a model for the oft-discussed lengthening of the contracts in the other metals. It was in fact discussed at length in the ensuing months (along with a possible delivery point for silver in New York), and it was put to the Board by the Committee in the spring of 1972. The Board came back with the suggestion that there be two contracts – one for three months and another for longer periods – and at the end of April a letter was sent to all Ring members enclosing copies of the proposed contract, and asking for their views. A Meeting of Subscribers (a rare occurrence on the LME) was held on 8 June 1972, at which attendance was on the whole disappointing. However, it was taken that those in attendance were in the main in favour of adopting the new proposal, and it is quite possible that the matter might have been taken further on the strength of this meeting.

Earlier in that year, however (in mid March, to be exact), there had occurred the collapse of an LME Ring member company, albeit not as a result of LME dealings, but of an ill-advised effort to establish a corner in a metal not traded and therefore un-hedgeable on the market. This sad affair somewhat dampened enthusiasm for anything like a contract with an even longer forward period than the existing seven months – at least until the Exchange had had time to take stock of its internal security arrangements – and the matter has not to date been revived.

The pound sterling floated
There is a body of opinion which holds that the level at which the UK authorities had held the parity of sterling before it was floated in July 1972 was too high to be realistic. However correct this view may be, the fact remains that the immediate result of the decision to free the pound to find its own level in the markets did at the outset bring about a somewhat abrupt devaluation. This alteration in parity was of course reflected in LME prices.

Silver responded to a greater degree than the other metals, prices rising by some 17% as compared with an average 5% for copper, lead and zinc. (The tin market thereupon became a more complicated affair, with the Buffer Stock Manager deciding to price in Malaysian dollars per picul rather than in pounds per tonne effectively for the time the Penang price took the lead over London.)

The silver surge

The seven months between mid August 1979 and mid March 1980 saw an unprecedented degree of movement in silver prices on Comex in New York which inevitably flowed over into the LME and the LSM in London. This was the brief era of the "Silver Bulls", of which the Hunt brothers William and Nelson Bunker became the most publicised. The story is a fascinating though complicated one, but being centred on Comex it is not properly material for treatment here *in extenso*.

However, as the drama unfolded, it did provide more than one salutary lesson for all concerned with the management of an orderly market. As such, it merits some reflection here. In brief, the situation arose (and was unwittingly encouraged to arise) where the market became almost totally polarised between a small group of "longs" and a small group of "shorts", the latter finding themselves increasingly distressed by a relentlessly rising price coupled with the insistence at least of some of the longs (the Hunts) on taking delivery rather than closing out their bought positions. That some of these deliveries were made by way of "EFPs", or Exchanges of Futures for Physical, made the position of the shorts somewhat less intolerable. By an EFP it is possible to deliver material which does not conform to the strict requirements of delivery under the official market contract.

The bullion dealers, too, were dragged almost willy-nilly into the fray, being themselves besieged by distress buyers of physical endeavouring to cover their short positions in a market where the longs appeared determined to call for delivery rather than to liquidate. The ensuing upsurge in the price was to an appreciable extent fuelled also by the selling activities of the dealers in physicals, who were finding that in order to be hedged they were being compelled to go short in the market at prices which were in the event climbing above those originally paid for the physical bullion. As the situation developed, the smaller speculators who would normally be counted on to balance the market to some extent by operating against the "professionals" were being inexorably driven out by a combination of escalating prices and of greatly increased margins imposed by a worried Comex management. Almost complete polarisation between the bulls and the short-hedging bullion dealers and producers was the inevitable outcome.

On the last trading day in December 1979 the Comex price for March delivery had approached $35 per ounce. It was to rise to $41.50 on 21 January 1980, and thereafter to remain in the mid $30s until the second week in March, by then the delivery month. Then began a sharp decline – in the event even more disastrous than the upsurge which had preceded it – to as low as $10.80 on "Silver Thursday" which was 27 March and the last trading day of the month. The bubble had burst, largely upon fears that the Hunt brothers were strapped for cash either to finance their holdings of silver and their continuing long positions or to meet a margin call said to be in excess of $100 million arising from this very decline in the price. To an extent, it could have been that the Hunts brought the market down upon their own heads by their unexpected offer of "silver bonds", promissory notes backed by silver from their hoard, to maintain financial liquidity. This was read, rightly or wrongly, as a signal that, being short of ready funds, they might start to off-load their holdings on to the market, which then "stood in wait" for them with progressively lower bids by the short-covering buyers.

The present position of silver on the LME
The attractiveness of silver as a means of hedging or of actually taking advantage of changes in currency parities has over the years sustained LME dealings at a respectably high level. But this aspect of the silver contract is certain to be affected, if not completely overshadowed, by opportunities offered by the Gold Futures Market and by the London International Financial Futures Exchange (LIFFE). It is, however, reasonably certain that the third essay at an LME silver contract is by now well enough established to continue as a successful market in its own right. The continuing use of silver in various industrial fields – notably in electronics – should ensure the contract's viability in the more traditional hedging sphere, where it also has a place alongside the physical trading on the LSM.

What will be interesting to see is whether the clearing house involvement in the gold market influences LME thinking towards a cleared silver contract (it has been thought of, and documented, before), perhaps with a return to the concept of trading the metal

111

further forward than three months. This possibility ought not to be ignored, especially in the light of the earlier abandonment of the uncleared seven-month silver contract.

Gold

Although gold is not traded in the Ring (there was a period when it might quite well have turned out so), the LME's involvement with the establishment of the London Gold Futures Market, and its half-ownership of its sponsoring company, justify at least a review of the events which led to the launching of this new contract.

There has always been a certain magic about gold, and it was therefore the most natural thing in the world for the LME to have thought seriously about a gold contract to add to its repertoire. Because of the connection between gold and money, however, persisting in one form or another even after all the reserve currency nations had abandoned the official Gold Standard, it was not permissible for private citizens in many western countries to possess gold other than as coin. This restriction was imposed in the interests of exchange control, to inhibit the "shunting" of capital by way of physical movements of bullion.

But the exchange control apparatus has been progressively dismantled and the first gold futures contract was launched – someshat surprisingly in Winnipeg, Ontario – in 1970. Though US citizens were active on this market, through a quirk of their own exchange control regulations they were not permitted to hold long positions on Winnipeg, these being tantamount to actual possession in the eyes of the authorities.

The restrictions in the United States were lifted at the end of 1974 and immediately gold futures contracts were introduced on Comex and the Mercantile Exchange in New York and on the Mercantile and the Board of Trade in Chicago. For technical reasons relating to the weights deliverable under these various contracts – which we need not go deeply into here – the Comex contract for one 100 troy ounce bar assaying not less than 0.995 fine very soon established a dominance which it has not lost.

In the UK exchange control restrictions were removed by the Conservative Government in the budget of 1979. Straightaway both the LME and the five members of the London Gold Market turned their attention to offering a futures market in gold in London. They went their separate ways, though each recognised from the outset that such a contract would have to be backed by a form of clearing house guarantee and have inbuilt provision for automatic "marking to market" based on daily price movements.

What is interesting to the student of commodity futures markets is the initial difference in approach of the two bodies to this aspect. Whereas the LME opted (one may imagine with a certain feeling of resignation) for the independent ICCH, the LGM appears to have gone some way down the path towards a mutual clearing corporation owned by the members of the market and with additional underwriting of its guarantee by a bank or consortium of banks. This in point of fact is the American method as used on the major exchanges in the United States.

It was not long before both the LME and the LGM began to appreciate that the possibility of there being two distinct gold futures contracts established in London was not really practical, or even desirable. (It is likely that their thoughts in the direction of a joint approach were stimulated by some discreet prodding from the Bank of England.) The London Gold Market Ltd had been incorporated as a company in which the five bullion houses which together make up the twice-daily London Gold "Fixings" each held 20% of the equity. A new company was then formed – The London Gold Futures Market Ltd – in which the capital of £10,000 was to be held 50:50 by the LGM Ltd and by the Metal Market & Exchange Company Ltd. Each "A" and "B" shareholder was to nominate three members to a board of six, with the Chair alternating regularly between an "A" director and a "B" director.

This produced an animal which was rather unusual in two ways. In the first place, its format set the LGFM Ltd up as a "deadlock" company in whose articles had to be written provisions for dealing with a situation where half the shareholders might be at odds with the other half. In the second place – and more significant – the new company is unique among the terminal market associations in London in being a company limited by shares rather than by guarantee. (The Metal Market & Exchange Company as we have already seen is also peculiar in that, although it is a company limited by shares, it has a somewhat "at one remove" relationship with the market itself, owing to the interposition of the LME Committee.)

The LGFM Ltd was not formally incorporated until June 1981, the delay being caused by a prolonged strike by civil servants at the time.

The London contract was set for delivery of lots of either 100 troy ounces in the form of a single bar (with limited weight tolerance) or of its nearest metric equivalent, i.e. three bars of 1 kg each. Trading was to be for the spot month and the next succeeding six months. In the early stages, when each party was looking independently at a possible gold contract, it appears to have been assumed by all that such a contract would be quoted in US dollars, which are, after all, the currency most widely used when pricing gold. Somewhere down the line, however, there was a change of heart by some of the contract's sponsors and sterling was put forward as the nominated currency. This proved a highly controversial choice and there followed prolonged and on occasion rather warm discussion, culminating in a meeting of LME subscribers in the Guildhall. The supporters of sterling won the day, however, and the contract was duly launched on 19 April 1982 after some periods of "dummy" trading in order to familiarise all concerned with the trading rules and procedures. In the event, after nine months of trading, the currency was changed to US dollars.

Almost as difficult of solution as the question of currency were those of the new market's membership and venue; by this time it was indeed taking shape as an exchange in its own right. Initial thinking had been, logically enough, that trading would be in the Ring of the LME, and that therefore it would be restricted to Ring members. No difficulty here, it would seem, since all but two of the five bullion houses were already Ring members, either directly or through associated companies. There would have been little problem in admitting the remaining two to Ring membership. But as the working party which had been set up continued its studies it became clear that trading on a more continuous basis than that which would have been possible between the LME's regular Rings was desirable, as would be the admission of further members with active connections in trading bullion.

Accordingly, new premises were sought and the decision was taken to extend membership beyond that of the LGM and the LME. A market Room was found in Plantation House (in fact, the erstwhile Arabica Coffee Market) and work was put in hand in the latter part of 1981 to ready it for trading the gold contract. Seating was extended from 33 to 38 – the maximum possible in the space available – and Floor membership of the LGFM could now be set at this limit. In the event, all members of the LGM and all Ring members of the LME made application for membership (for an initial purchase of a seat at £55,000) as did some 15 who were not members of either body but who matched the criteria laid down for

Floor membership. Of these latter, eight were admitted, not without some understandable heartache amongst those who were not.

And so London's first gold futures market was opened formally by the Lord Mayor, and trading commenced on 19 April 1982 with August as the first delivery month. The new market by then had altered radically from the initial concept; it had become a more or less complete facsimile of a traditional "soft" commodity exchange, cleared by the ICCH and complete with regular Calls to Market, continuous trading throughout two daily sessions of three hours each and with no kerb or off-market trading allowed under the contract.

If some of the more traditionally oriented LME Ring members were somewhat surprised at finding themselves trading in such an ambience (or even to be trading gold at all), they very rapidly acclimatised.

Other precious metals

The creation of the LGFM, and its close connection with the LME through shareholding and Board representation, could well make it less likely that trading in other precious metals will be introduced on the LME. However, the *modus operandi* of the LGFM with day-long trading could of itself make if difficult if not impossible to trade another contract on the same floor.

It is open to speculation therefore on which exchange a contract in platinum or gold coin, for example, might be introduced. Each of these could be regarded as a contender for inclusion in London's repertoire of futures markets, and platinum futures are already traded on the New York Mercantile Exchange. The sudden and unexpected imposition of VAT on gold coin bought and sold (as distinct from being offered as legal tender for the purchase of goods) in 1982 makes the idea of a formal exchange with its own VAT provision along the lines of those for other commodities quite an attractive proposition.

"Special" metals

There has been much written and spoken about a number of other metals, notably cobalt and the so-called "strategic" metals. While some of this could be rated no higher than optimism – or opportunism – on the part of those with a knowledge of them and a desire to capitalise on such knowledge, it should be remembered that the

115

topic of establishing some sort of bourse for trading these and the Minor Metals is not a new one. In the early 1970s the LME Committee set up a Minor Metals Sub-committee to look into it in depth, but at the time no positive steps were taken to further the matter.

But it must remain a tempting possibility. The setting up – space permitting – of an informal market-place for individual dealings could well be a first step towards one or more new Ring contracts if anticipated turnover seems to justify them and any technical problems in writing the contracts are overcome. This, after all, is how lead and zinc were both brought into the LME.

PART THREE
Trading on the LME

10

The Ring

Background

We have already seen how the development of arrivals dealing made it possible for at least some form of forward trading to be carried out. It has also been maintained, probably logically, that the advance announcement of the arrival dates of ships gave the LME its unique method of trading in days rather than delivery months. And we have noted how the physical nature of base metals – their durability and comparative freedom from corrosion in store – permitted the in-warehouse contract providing for collection on any day. There was no pressing need for conversion and fabrication of the metal on its discharge from vessel.

The development of the standard contracts, of the system of dealing only in approved brands of metal under the contracts, went a long way to assuage doubts as to what precisely a buyer might be bidding for in terms of quality. (This process was not a rapid one, nor is it in any way final. LME contracts have been and will continue to be subject to review as to brand and specification in the light of the changing world of fabrication techniques and end-user requirements.) The standard contract, combined with the now universal three-month maximum forward period, gives scope for a very rapid way of actually doing business. There is no need to bargain over quality or grade: the buyer knows the spectrum of brands from which would be drawn the one for delivery to him. As to location, he knows the siting of the listed delivery points. He need only to chaffer over price and prompt date.

Dealing in or around the Ring chalked on the floor of the Exchange had been banned in 1881, but it was reinstated in April 1882 and has been continuous ever since, save only for the periods of market closure during the two World Wars. When Ring trading was again permitted in 1882, dealing times were notably brief: from 11.50 a.m. to 12 noon and from 3.40 p.m. to 3.50 p.m. To those, and they are not a few, who feel that today's Ring sessions with attendant kerb trading are still too short, these earlier times must appear to have been almost unworkable. In point of fact they were very soon increased, and, when for a time dealings in pig iron were also included, the practice arose of separating the dealings in each metal to individual 10-minute periods. Though iron has long since ceased to be traded on the LME, the separate Rings remain, now reorganised into five-minute periods for each metal.

In the 1890s the Secretary and his handbell made their debut in the Ring. A clang of the bell and a cry of "Copper, gentlemen, copper" commenced the day's proceedings. After the allotted time, checked on the Secretary's watch, came a further ring of the bell and the announcement of the next metal. This system survived until the present one of electronic timing was introduced, accompanied first by the harsh clangour of a bell, and latterly by a discreet yet sufficiently audible chime. Now the Secretary's rostrum is used officially only for calling out the daily prices and the making of announcements. The levying of fines from those careless enough to be heard bidding or offering after the bell is established practice; on occasions when one of the doyens of the Ring is so caught out there is a general and joyous cry of "Pay up!" from all present.

In the early days lead and spelter (zinc) were traded separately from copper and tin in a smaller Ring of their own and the metals were not all traded in the one Ring until after the First World War. This merging was made possible with the introduction of standard contracts in lead and zinc, which rendered unnecessary the erstwhile bargaining over grade as well as price and prompt. Actually, zinc was traded on a system of fortnightly prompts as distinct from days until the middle of the inter-war period.

Trading in the Ring

To the uninitiated, the Ring towards the close of an active session must seem to possess most of the attributes of Bedlam. There is observable no shape or formality, nor any apparent master of ceremonies such as an auctioneer or the Call Chairman who presides over formal trading on the soft commodity markets. The impression is one of an easy informality contrasting strangely on occasions with real tension. All this is because the Ring is self-governing: there are those in authority, and there is in fact a definite and scrupulously observed protocol. But each is embodied in the Ring itself and therefore neither is immediately apparent to a stranger.

During the quarter of an hour or so before the time set for trading to commence, all who are to be concerned foregather in the foyer of the Exchange with its examples of the metals in their display cases along with early documents and an array of golfing trophies (golf is endemic to the LME). They pass the time of day with each other and exchange comment on the state of the pre-Market and on any other factor or item of news which may affect the tenor of that day's trading. As with any gathering of professionals used to working together, there is also a sub-current of badinage on subjects not detectably connected with the business in hand.

Traders and clerks pass through the door leading to the Ring. Once inside, they man the booths which surround the Ring itself and establish telephone contact with their offices. Time was when others who were not actually involved with trading were also able to stand between the booths and the seats which formed the Ring in the Whittington Avenue Rooms. This was looked on as a somewhat mixed blessing; physical encounters between visitors and harrassed clerks scurrying between their trader and their booth were the order of the day. Now only those directly concerned may enter the Ring and all others are banished upstairs to the viewing gallery; this is more comfortable (and probably safer) than standing on the actual periphery, but gives nothing like the same feeling of being a part of the proceedings.

The LME staff check the calendars which show the day's date and that for three months forward, and one of them stations himself unobtrusively by the rostrum ready to activate the bell for timing the Rings and the illumination of the symbols for each of the metals mounted on the walls with the calendars and the inevitable clocks.

Though the venerable benches from the "old" Ring have been pensioned off and replaced by more commodious ones, the system of numbering each place and allotting it to a named company for the use of its traders continues. Clerks with notebooks at the ready stand behind their traders, prepared to record each deal done by them. There was a time when it was considered essential for each clerk to be able to record every trade, but perhaps things were not so hectic then.

THE LONDON METAL EXCHANGE

Despite the hours of pre-Market preparation that go into working out approximately (by the exacting LME standards of accuracy) where prices will emerge, the first Ring is invariably a fairly tentative encounter. A bid will be made – "I'll give two, three months" – and a counter offer "I'll sell at a half." Other voices join in and for a few moments there will be a flurry of vocal activity. Then, more than likely, there will be an almost embarrassed silence during which a cough unstifled may raise a laugh and a cry of "How much?"

As though by collective telepathy, the closing seconds before each bell bring forth a mini-crescendo of calls. Then there is a general movement as some traders leave their seats to talk for a few brief moments before resuming their places if they have "something to do" in the next metal, and the clerks commence their rounds checking trades done in the preceding Ring.

And so each of the metals is traded for five minutes, silver being taken out of sequence during the first Ring in order that the first LME silver dealings may be done before the Bullion Market Fixing. The second silver Ring is taken after the day's fix is known. Each metal follows the same common pattern as to procedure, and after nickel the Room clears while each in his individual way savours or works through the all too short five minutes of interval before the second Ring commences.

"I'll give Oh"

In common with other outcry markets, the LME has adopted set minimum price fluctuations, or steps between quotes. These vary from metal to metal: 25p in the case of lead and zinc, 50p for copper, £1 for tin and one-tenth of a new penny for silver are examples. Everyone is presumed to know the "big figure" and only the last digit or fraction is called, although it is traditional to call the whole sum at the commencement of Ring trading in each metal. Thus an offer, say, of £435.50 per tonne for zinc could be called as "I'll sell at a half" and a counter-bid as "I'll give a quarter" if £435.25 is being bid. On the round figure, what easier than to call "I'll give" – or "I'll sell at" – "Oh"?

As to amounts of metal, since the warehouse warrant is standard, these are quoted either as "I'll sell two warrants at five", or more briefly as "I'll sell two at five." "Cash" means a trade for delivery and settlement the day following, and dates are called as such for trades on any market day up to three months forward. In actual practice, the calling of intermediate days is now confined in most

122

part to dealing in "carries" (which we shall look at later) and rarely used in straightforward buying and selling where cash and three months are the typical calls.

"How much?"

But there are occasions where a seller does not specify the amount he has to offer. Obviously, if he has a large tonnage to sell, to announce this and so reveal his hand could well make buyers chary and depress bid prices against him. What to do? An order to sell say 2000 tonnes "at the close" may in many circumstances be far from easy to fulfil, should the market be unresponsive. Equally, the order to dispose of the 2000 tonnes "at best" may tempt a seller to hold his order until it is too late to move it in one package in one Ring. Faced with a large selling order, therefore, the dealer may simply call an offer and await developments. A cry of "How much?" from a bidder compels that bidder to take up to – but no more than – 20 warrants (500 tonnes of copper, lead or zinc) at the offered price. Should the seller not have that much to dispose of, then the bidder must be ready to take the balance up to the full 20 warrants (the "unfilled balance") from whoever immediately offers it at the price. Of course, the converse applies when a seller calls "How much?" in response to a bid.

A call of "Yes!", *tout court,* in response to an unquantified bid or offer obliges the caller to take or sell up to 20 lots from or to the other party. However, here he does not have to sell or take any unfilled balance if the 20 lots are not completed. He deals, in short, only with the one other trader and need not be at the disposal of others as well.

The LME has its conventions here, too, and they are universally observed. In the case outlined above, and faced with a bid of "How much?", the offeror must not sell, say, only two warrants at the price (having in so doing satisfied himself that the demand is there) and then offer again at a higher price. Were he to do this, he would in effect be holding the rest of the Ring to ransom. Of course, if seller A offers and sells, and is followed by seller B offering (and selling) at a higher price, then seller A is free to offer whatever else he has now to dispose of at the newly established going price.

To make assurance double sure in such cases, both buyers and sellers are encouraged by the authorities to call firmly "I withdraw." This has the effect of converting a seller or buyer over (that is, one who still has something to do) into an uncommitted dealer still waiting for the right price at which to make his own offer or bid. It thus frees the Ring for further calling, at above or below the price at which the withdrawal was made.

Dealers in the Ring act as both buyers and sellers, and it is quite in order (and quite logical) to appear as both in one and the same call. A trader who calls "I'll give three and sell at five" is taken as meaning nothing more nor less than that – he will trade either way at the price he has named for either way. He must not therefore claim that his offer (at five) cancelled his bid by virtue of having been made later. Should he wish to withdraw either offer or bid, he must clearly do so, or be prepared to deal in accordance with either.

First come, first served

In a situation such as has been described above, there is a measure of protection for seller A. The Rules of the LME do in fact expressly state that no other seller may offer at a higher price (nor buyer bid a lower) than that at which there is at the time another bidder or offeror. Seller B should therefore be certain that A has completed his own sale before himself coming in to offer at a higher price. The principle of first come, first served is scrupulously observed, and an unsatisfied seller over at £250 has legitimate cause for grievance if another offers at £252 the while. This is of particular importance when the official prices are being assessed in the second Ring of official trading, and where it may well be of great importance to a seller (say) to be able to confirm that the official sellers' price was indeed that at which – on the bell – he was a seller over. He must not be put in baulk by another offeror calling a higher price whilst he still has metal to sell at the figure at which he has already offered.

Buyers, too, have their own measure of protection. Although the call "I'll take yours" by a bidder to an offeror is officially frowned upon, it does indicate readiness to buy in quantity if the metal is on offer. An offeror ought therefore not to stop – as we have seen – at (say) four warrants only sold to one bidder, and then after a discreet pause recommence offering at a higher price. The bidder ought to have his chance to buy what is on offer up to his own limit (provided such a tonnage is available) at the offer price originally called. If the bidder requires more, then naturally he will be ready to bid again to another seller.

Where an offer is made, and there are several bidders who by various cries of "Yes!" or "How much?" (accompanied in a busy Ring by expressive gestures indicating a strong willingness to buy), the offeror should either sell to whoever clearly was the first to bid, or parcel out the tonnage fairly amongst all. Hence, "Two for you, two for you and one for you" after an offer of five warrants has been accepted by three simultaneous bidders.

No trading limits

Minimum price fluctuations have been mentioned. It is important to note that, although these are adhered to, there is no equivalent on the LME to the maximum price fluctuation which may give rise to a "limit move" on certain of the other markets, such as the London Gold Futures Market. A limit move occurs when the price bid or offered exceeds or falls short of a datum – usually the close of the previous day or trading session – by a pre-ordained amount. In the event of a limit move all trading save that in the spot month ceases for a set time. The duration of this pause in trading varies from market to market where such limits are imposed, and when dealings are resumed the call which brought about the limit move becomes the new datum.

There is discussion from time to time on the LME as to the desirability of such a procedure, but it is highly unlikely that it will be instituted there. The arguments in favour are that first of all it gives members time to advise their clients of the state of the market and to make any necessary adjustments to the margins of those clients, as well as their own to the clearing house in a cleared market; and that secondly it affords a welcome "cooling-off" period in what by implication must be a somewhat volatile market. Arguments against are that nobody likes, and in times of high interest rates few can afford, to be locked in to a situation until trading resumes; and also that in a heavily moving market such a cessation of trading makes the execution of stop-loss orders very difficult.

The authorities on the LME do, however, have the right to impose limits on trading *ad hoc* should they decide that conditions in the market so warrant. This action is very rarely taken, being considered only in the most extreme conditions and only after much quite proper agonising by the Board and the Committee. In December 1973 a decision was taken to request Ring members not to open new bought positions in zinc at a time when a supply crisis in a particular grade of zinc was making the whole market in that metal a most unsettled affair. The restriction was very short-lived and the bulk of the trading barely affected. In the spring of 1982, with all the symptoms displayed of an impending squeeze in tin, a maximum was put on the backwardation over any 24-hour period. This, too, was a brief interruption to trading and one which did enable distress buyers covering short positions in the then very unstable tin market to do so without undue penalty.

Executions

Much has been written, and said, both in favour of and against the latitude which the principals' contract allows in the price made for execution of an order. An exact match of the client's desired price and that actually obtainable at any time on the market is not always possible on the LME, nor on any other exchange. However, with full price transparency afforded by the insistence on other exchanges that all dealings be "brought to the floor" and the system of timing all such dealings, it is open to the client to check what prices were at the time his order was executed. The extent of off-market trading on the LME militates against such complete price transparency.

One must bear in mind, however, the LME's avowed intent to be and to remain primarily a delivery market for the trade. Here, such latitude can work very much to the client's benefit. For example, he may be a fabricator needing to execute a market order for closing a hedge. This has to be done on a given day in order that he is not exposed, with either side of his dealings (physical or market) uncovered. The Ring member receiving the order may find himself unable to attract a counterparty for the date in question, or to attract one at the right price. In such circumstances he may either take the client's order on his own book, or trade the nearest practicable date and price and himself cover any discrepancy.

The second Ring

When dealers reassemble after the interval for the second Ring in each metal (with silver here being taken last of all), the atmosphere is noticeably different. On the last bid and offer called in each of these Rings will depend the official LME prices which will then stand as world prices for the ensuing 24 hours. Small wonder, then, that a measure of tension can be felt, or that the closing seconds of each Ring are marked by an increase in both the volume and the tempo of the calling.

After the bell has sounded, one of the LME staff visits each of the three members of the Quotations Committee at his place in the Ring in order to obtain his opinion as to the final bid and offer made as the bell started ringing. After the close of silver the three "quoters" foregather in a corner of the Room for a final check amongst themselves, and to agree that in every case last bids and offers were indeed representative of the tone of prices in each Ring, not being pitched too high or too low in relation to the overall trend. This done, the Secretary or his assistant mounts the rostrum, the bell rings for silence, and the day's prices are ritually read aloud: cash and three months buyers and sellers for each metal.

Should there be a protest (and they are neither infrequent nor frowned on) the dealer making it stands and voices his objection: "Gentlemen, I would like to protest the three months buyers price for lead. I was bidding three right up to the bell" – or whatever his objection may be. A brief conference by the Quotations Committee follows, possibly accompanied by a groundswell of "Quite right!" from those seated around the Ring, and the decision is made there and then. Either the price is altered in deference to the protest or it is confirmed by a polite but firm "No change, gentlemen."

The tone for dealings, and prices, in the second Ring has been set in the course of pre-Market and first Ring dealings. An occasional exception here is silver, where the bullion brokers' fix is known after the first, but as a rule before the second, Ring on the LME. After the interval, therefore, it is likely that more precision (smaller brackets between buyers and sellers) will be combined with a higher degree of intensity. This applies in particular to business done on behalf of those clients, and they are the majority, who are directly concerned with the trade and to whom a shift in the LME price over the next 24 hours is a matter of great consequence. Pricing an intake or closing a hedge, when several hundreds of tons may be involved, can often be a pretty critical matter. It is here in the second Ring that individual techniques amongst the dealers, or techniques adapted to suit conditions, are observable to the experienced eye. Some may choose to contain themselves until they feel the *moment critique* has arrived, and then make their bid or offer; others (or the same men with a different set of conditions to deal with) may to some extent make a market by moving in and out frequently during the five minutes. All naturally seek to avoid disclosing any more of their hand than may be absolutely inescapable.

Each dealer's "card" which he carries with him into the Ring shows his positions long or short for dates where such positions exist, and it is his responsibility to make the necessary moves in order to maintain or to balance those positions at the most advantageous prices possible. Frequently an instruction conveyed in the

127

THE LONDON METAL EXCHANGE

course of a Ring may entail alteration of a planned approach, calling for extremely rapid reassessment if time (and money) are not to be lost before the adaptation is put into effect. Five minutes can be a very short time indeed, but its very brevity compels decision. In this way there is probably more intense and furious concentration devoted to the bids and offers which lead to the day's prices on the LME than applies in any other pricing forum.

The kerb

Kerb trading is a facility which, though not peculiar to the LME, is not often seen in other commodity markets. Where transactions have to be registered before being cleared by a central clearing house, it is in fact difficult to accommodate. The kerb is – or was, as its name implies – an overflow market where members did indeed at one time stand on the pavement outside a by now closed Room and continue trading. This was the case particularly in the early years of the LME when trading in the Room was restricted to very brief periods. It could easily be that a member had an unusually large tonnage to trade and simply was not able to place it all within the confines of official trading without either over-burdening the market or causing prices to run against him, to his or his client's detriment. What to do, then, but continue to bid or offer on a more direct basis afterwards?

But the LME authorities took the view that too much kerb trading might give the practice an undue importance, to the extent even of undermining the authoritativeness of the official prices. Accordingly, they made continuous and determined efforts to restrain unofficial dealings, but these met with little success. Closure of the Room and an enforced evacuation sharply at the end of official trading merely led to a market in the street outside which often aroused adverse comment from occupiers of neighbouring offices; so finally the authorities bowed to the inevitable and set aside a limited period after each official session for "kerb" trading within the Room.

The practice continues, though today members trade on the kerb market from their seats, or from places identifiable with them, rather than stand – as they did within living memory – in a close circle around the motif in the centre of the Ring. All metals are traded simultaneously during kerb trading periods with no bell or coloured illuminated symbols.

The kerb has several purposes. As we have seen, it affords a welcome and often necessary continuation of trading for the dealer with many commitments, or many tons to dispose of on one date. It also provides the opportunity for the general tidying-up of market books (and levelling as far as may be of positions) after a day's trading. Perhaps most important though is the facility which it provides for members to trade in intermediate dates as necessary between the extremes of cash and three months. To attempt to trade such a date during Ring dealings can be frustrating with no bidders to an offer (or offerors for a bid) for one particular day. And yet a deal on that day may be important to a hedging strategy, for example. On the kerb it is much less difficult to trade these dates even by "knitting" a deal together by means of judicious swaps and the offering of terms just outside the running range of prices being called in Ring dealings. Another example of the flexibility afforded by the principals' contract, perhaps!

It is of course more difficult in kerb dealings to keep track of prices in all the metals at the same time than in formalised Ring trading, and in consequence a trader must be on his guard against the possibility of overbidding or undercalling, both technical breaches of the trading rules of the LME. But practice makes, if not always perfect, skilful. Confusing as it is to the inexperienced, the kerb is a busy time for the senior trader.

Afternoon trading is in a great many respects very much akin to kerb dealings. True, the formality of dealing in separate Rings for the metals is resumed, but the atmosphere and the manner in which trading is conducted is more redolent of the informal atmosphere of the kerb than of the official dealings which preceded it. To a great extent afternoon dealings are therefore but a continuation of the morning's kerb, but there is a difference. By the time the LME has commenced its afternoon session, the Commodity Exchange (Comex) in New York is also in session. There is a considerable volume of business done in copper and silver by way of arbitrage between the two markets, and on occasions when Comex has taken a particularly definite line this can have an appreciable influence on the later LME dealings. In fact, anything so important as the closing of Comex on a limit movement up or down can have repercussions lasting beyond that day's afternoon market on the LME. Although by LME standards the amount of physical delivery business done on the New York market is very small, the amount of investment business and arbitrage with London is considerable. It follows therefore that any major movement or change in the day's trading pattern coming from that quarter will have its own reflection in LME dealings, possibly into the following day.

If afternoon trading on the LME tends to merge into the later kerb without appreciable change in tempo or atmosphere it is because the whole is effectively more of a kerb than a formalised market. Where both afternoon Ring trading and kerb come into their own is precisely when a development on the other side of the world has upset the pattern of the day's trading. Then they can act as a most necessary relief valve for the easing of any pressures generated, and in so doing provide a smoother start for the next day's official dealings.

It is a prelude for the morrow, rather than as any sort of coda to the actual day's trading, that these sessions ought to be regarded.

In sum . . .

The LME takes a justifiable pride in being a "continuous market". This presupposes that dealings should be capable of being conducted throughout the day with maximum contact member to member and with minimum interruption. But, as is the case on a call market, there has to be a time during the 24 hours when the day's prices are set and crystallised in a disciplined manner and in the presence of all those members who are concerned with the making of them. In this context the Rings of the LME and in particular the second Rings in the morning session equate with the Call to Market in other exchanges.

As such, trading in the Ring might almost be said to justify a work of reference all to itself. Unfortunately, such a work would perforce have to be continually in course of revision. The identity of the market, and its liveliness as a living and developing organism in constant growth and movement is never more forcefully shown than by the changing face of the Ring.

11

Hedging on the LME

Hedging may aptly be described as a matter of holding up a mirror to physical trading. In precisely the way in which an ordinary optical mirror reverses the positions of left and right, so does a "classic" hedge reverse the positions of bought and sold. The word "classic" is emphasised because, whilst the transposition of images in an optical mirror is instant, the equivalent in a hedge on the LME is gradual, and may take any time up to the prescribed forward dealing period. There always exists the means of so adjusting the mirror as to keep the image constant – or as nearly constant as makes no matter – during this time.

In essence, a purchase of physical material for pricing on a given date in the future may be matched by a hedging sale of a like amount prompt the same date, and vice versa. Because of certain technical vagaries such as changes in the going rate of backwardation or contango, there exists both time and scope for a hedge to be modified from what may have been "classical" at the time of its opening to what may by now have become more appropriate as conditions develop during its currency. (It is really rather unfair, in this context, to separate simple buying and selling forward from the complementary technique of lending and borrowing, but for clarity's sake they will here be treated separately.)

Some of the more basic ways in which hedging – forward selling or buying – may be used in order to minimise potential loss will be the subject of this chapter. Meanwhile, certain basic principles should be mentioned:

1. It is not necessary to limit hedging operations to cover the actual brands being bought or sold. As long as the producer prices on the LME, or his prices are so worked out as to move in line with the LME, then his brands are capable of being hedged on the market, even though they may not actually be delivered there. In the same way, any premium which may be commanded by a given brand in the physical market need not affect hedging, since it can be taken into account separately as are other incidental costs.

2. Because of the LME's facility for trading in days rather than in delivery months only, it is possible to open or close a hedge on any market day within the permitted forward trading period.

3. The fact that the great majority of producer to consumer contracts are of longer duration than the standard LME three months contract need not be an inhibiting factor. It is possible, by what is known on the LME as "borrowing" or "lending" – buying nearby and selling forward or vice versa – to roll a market position forward into another period of up to three months: thus maintaining the hedge in position.

4. In the event of a brand registered on the LME being hedged, a possible alternative to closing the hedge by a sale or purchase on the market would be taking up or delivering the actual warrants.

5. In a thin market, such as exists from time to time in certain of the metals or grades, the fact that a buyer or a seller for the precise date at the precise price may not be forthcoming is no bar. The flexibility of the LME principals' contract enables the Ring member carrying out the transaction to exercise a measure of discretion in his execution of it.

Given these essentials, some examples of how various hedging transactions are actually carried out on the LME may now be considered. In these examples, simplicity has been the main aim, in order to demonstrate how the transactions work. Details about other extraneous costs and cash flow are omitted, since these are by no means common to all.

Selling or "short" hedge

A merchant buys 100 tonnes of pig lead at a price based on the current LME settlement price, for shipment and eventual sale to a customer who will buy it – also at a price based on the LME settlement price – on delivery at his works. The merchant knows what he has paid his own supplier for the lead, and knows, or can with reasonable accuracy predict, his costs of freight and insurance in transit. What neither party can know at this juncture is what the price of lead will be when it is due for delivery and pricing at the customer's works.

To cover himself, the merchant will sell 100 tonnes forward (short) on the LME, prompt the date on which the physical material is due for delivery and pricing. This forward sale will be made at the price obtaining on the LME for that date.

On delivery of the metal to his customer, the merchant will buy in on the LME in order to close out his position. This he will do at the LME cash price on the day, which will also be the price upon which his sale of physical to his customer will be based. Depending on the movement in the lead price between the dates of opening and closing out the hedge, he will either receive or have to pay a market difference on the LME side of the deal. This difference will be the reverse of whatever difference there is between his original purchase price for the physical lead and the price he receives from his customer. The two will balance (give or take whatever contango or backwardation there may have been at the time) and the merchant is covered against any adverse movement in the price of lead between inception and completion of the deal with his customer, and thus need not try to take this movement into account when arriving at his own costs and margin of profit on the deal.

Physical	*LME*
Buys 100 tonnes lead at price based on LME settlement price on date of purchase (£295) for delivery on a date within coming 3 months.	Sells 100 tonnes prompt on date of delivery of physical, at LME price for that date (£300).
On date of delivery to customer's works, sells to him at the day's LME settlement price (£310).	Buys in on the Market at same price (£310), to close out his forward sale.
Extra profit of £15 per tonne.	Market loss of £10 per tonne.

In this example, a £5 contango was assumed, and this operated in the merchant's favour as he was able to make his forward sale at a higher price than his purchase price on the Market. Selling forward into a backwardation has the opposite effect.

Had lead prices declined by £15 per tonne, the effect would have been that the merchant would have lost this amount on sale to the customer of the physical. He would, however, have recovered £20

133

on the LME side of the deal. Once again, the contango would have worked in his favour.

(There is a limit to the extent of a contango, but a backwardation is both without limit and very unpredictable as to its extent. For this reason, hedging into a back is treated here separately.)

The physical and the LME sides of the hedging example above are quite separate, and as the lead sold and subsequently repurchased on the LME was not intended for actual delivery to the customer, its brand and the location of the warehouse are alike immaterial.

Buying or "long" hedge

A maker of brass rod for use in engineering is asked to quote for an order involving a tonnage of copper and zinc (the main constituents of brass). The date of delivery of the completed order is to be agreed on his customer's acceptance of his quotation. The price of the metal is the largest element in the calculation which the rod maker must now do in order to arrive at a price to quote to his customer, and in his quotation he must cover himself for whatever he must pay his own supplier for that metal. This purchase will be on a date in the future, and at prices which will be based on the as yet unknown LME settlement prices for copper and zinc ruling at that date.

The rod maker will buy copper and zinc forward on the LME (up to the amounts needed to replenish his own stock) at the current LME price for the date on which the replacement material will be required. The prices to which he has now committed himself on the LME on these forward purchases will be used in his quotation as the cost to him of the actual metal to be used in meeting his customer's needs. To these he will add his other calculated costs and his margin.

On the day he is to receive and price his replacement material he will sell against forward purchases on the LME and close out his position there. If copper and zinc prices have risen, he will have in his favour a market difference which will offset the higher prices he must now pay to his supplier. Should prices have fallen, he will have forgone the benefit of such a fall, since the Market difference will be against him. However, in either case he will have been able to cost the whole operation from the outset without anxiety as to physical prices in the future, and to have made a firm quote to his own customer.

Had the prices of copper and zinc moved in different directions,

134

the "swings and roundabouts" effect of hedging would still have helped the rod maker cover himself in this way.

Physical	LME
Copper Allows £1090 per tonne as price of copper content, in preparing his quotation.	Buys 75 tonnes prompt 3 months hence at 3 months price of £1090 per tonne.
Buys 75 tonnes from supplier 3 months later at settlement price (£1050).	Sells at settlement price (£1050) to close out his bought position.
Profit of £40 per tonne.	Market loss of £40 per tonne.
Zinc Allows £465 per tonne as price of zinc content, in preparing his quotation.	Buys 25 tonnes prompt 3 months hence at 3 months price of £465 per tonne.
Buys 25 tonnes from supplier 3 months later at settlement price (£480).	Sells at settlement price (£480) to close out his bought position.
Loss of £15 per tonne.	Market profit of £15 per tonne.

The full three months period need not of course be used: if it had suited the rod maker to have used an intermediate date and price (or different ones for each metal) he could have done so. The essence is to use whatever forward price is applicable as the basic price in arriving at his quotation.

Selling hedge by a producer

A producer may sell three months forward on the LME to hedge his own sales of physical to his customers, regardless of whether these are effected on the LME or, more probably, direct. On the prompt date he buys in to close his hedge and, if prices have fallen, his LME profit will counterbalance reduced revenue from sales of physical. If prices have risen, then the reverse occurs, but the producer has been able to cover himself against the possibility of a fall. (If he produces a brand registered on the LME, he may deliver physical on to the Market rather than buy in, to close his hedge.)

On a falling market, it is reasonable to assume that there will be a contango, and this is an added incentive to forward selling on the market by a producer. The following example illustrates this.

Assume a 10% per annum contango.
Today cash is £600 and 3 months is £615 (+2.5% of £600). In 3 months' time cash is, say, £560 and 3 months now is £574.
A producer selling on the basis of the LME settlement price then receives only £560 for physical, but makes £55 on closing his hedge at £615 per tonne.

135

Unhedged, the producer would have seen the cash price decline by £40 and been powerless to cover himself against the decline.

It is vital that the producer times the closing of his hedge to correspond with pricing of his physical sale, and the problem of monthly average prices may arise in this connection. Most producers' sales contracts if based on the LME use as their basis the average LME cash price over the month in which delivery is made. (Back-pricing is left out of account here, but covered in Chapter 14 on pricing.)

If he has enough to sell, the producer may spread his forward hedging sales so as to include an equal proportion of the monthly total on each market day of the month, and then buy in on the corresponding days of the month in which his physical delivery is to be priced. This would presuppose a monthly tonnage of at least one warrant, 25 tonnes, per market day. In general practice, however, both the forward sales and repurchases are made in one or a few tranches over the month.

Selling forward is therefore attractive on a falling market and with a contango ruling. It is to a large extent unnecessary in a market where prices are rising strongly, and it becomes unprofitable when a backwardation emerges. The producer, or his LME broker, needs therefore to watch for signals that might forecast an upward turn in prices (i.e. a contraction in LME stocks) or a significant diminution of the contango. He will then have to decide whether such signs indicate a possibly lasting trend, or are symptoms only of a temporary spasm of bullishness.

Conversely, in a market which has been rising and where the producer has been content to profit by sales based on an increasing monthly average, a watchful eye should be kept on any signs that this situation is likely to change and prices to commence a downward trend. If he reads these signs aright, the producer should institute a programme of forward hedging sales at the higher levels now obtaining, in order to cushion himself against the possibility of falling revenue from sales of physical in the months to come. It may well be in his interest here to sell even into a backwardation, if that is seen to be in the process of diminishing.

In view of the fact that the majority of producer contracts are for periods in excess of the three months LME contract, the need arises for hedging positions to be on correspondingly longer terms. They can be rolled forward by means of borrowing against a hedge sale and lending against a hedge purchase.

Hedging by an importer or fabricator

Importers rarely buy physical on the LME, because under the system of sellers' options as to deliveries there can be no guarantee that they will receive the brands they require, either for their own use as fabricators or for onward sale to their customers. Indeed, some of these brands may not even be registered on the LME. Just the same, the importer who is in all probability buying his physical from producers on long-term contract, providing a steady rate of deliveries and pricings, wishes to keep his own purchase and sales ledgers as nearly in balance as possible for cash-flow reasons. They are not automatically self-balancing one with the other: his customers will almost certainly not themselves be buying and pricing as regularly as he is, and when possible they will opt to price at a time when the market is low, or moving in their favour.

When the importer's bought position exceeds his sold position by an appreciable margin, he may bring it into balance by selling the surplus forward on the LME. When sales have exceeded purchases, or when these forward contracts become prompt, he will repurchase them and close his position. (Note that he does not as a rule intend to deliver on the LME against these forward sales.) In the event that some or all of the forward sales are prompt whilst the importer is still long (overbought) he may roll them forward on the Exchange by borrowing, i.e. buying them in, and reselling them further forward.

So far, so good; and if there is a contango then the premium receivable on the forward sales will go all or a large part of the way towards covering finance and storage costs of any surplus physical he is holding in stock. (As copper is traded on the LME in warrants of 25 tonnes each, and as pricing is usually on the average LME price over the month of delivery, complete back-to-back precision is not feasible; however, an importer with a large enough throughput will tend to average out over a period.)

Faced with the need to buy on the LME in order to match sales made outside, and in a contango, the importer would close out first the nearer dates on his outstanding LME forward sales in order to pay the least possible contango on the purchases. This would also enable him to keep his options open as to the remoter dates against which a closing-out purchase might be made at an advantageous price on a fall in market values.

Once again, the emergence of a backwardation throws these calculations out of gear. The importer or fabricator is faced with the purely subjective decision as to whether there is likely to be a fall in the price of his physical purchases which would make what now amounts to paying a penalty on his forward sales (into the backwardation) worth the paying. An extreme backwardation rarely endures for very long, since its existence at all is a symptom of a shortage of nearby physical. This would either be remedied at source (settlement of a strike, resuming operations at a mine which has suffered some setback) or the shortage could well compel the supplier himself to cut back on deliveries. Unfortunately, though, resumption of supplies and disappearance of the backwardation invariably bring in their wake a sharp fall in prices: "The bigger the back, the greater the fall" is a Market truism.

Should there be signs of the likelihood of an approaching back-wardation – a decline in LME stocks is a reliable omen – the importer or fabricator would be advised to commence a programme of closing his forward sales in order to avoid or minimise the need to pay the back should he close out too late.

Summing up

The main purpose of hedging is to negate or at least minimise losses on purchases and sales of physical metal. Any extra profit which may be forthcoming ought to be regarded as a bonus – a lollipop – and not sought after as a profit in its own right. In essence, the profit or loss arising on a hedging transaction may be summarised as being the difference between cash and forward on the LME when the hedge is first set up (excepting here the circumstances outlined in the example on pages 134–135 where cash did not figure in the calculation).

For a selling hedge, the profit or loss will be forward price minus cash price multiplied by tonnage dealt. For a buying hedge it will be cash price minus forward price multiplied by tonnage. A contango assists a selling hedge therefore and a backwardation a buying one.

Once opened, the hedge need not be slavishly kept open until the original prompt date. Advantage may be taken, and frequently is by the more sophisticated users of the Market, of momentary changes in prices in order to effect a partial closure, followed more often than not by reinstatement under more favourable conditions. The most important factor governing the option to do this would in all probability be a change in the relationship of cash to forward (changing contango or backwardation), rather than a change in prices overall. Taking advantage of such a change in the pattern would involve the use of carries (lending or borrowing on the Market), which will be studied in more detail in the next chapter.

12

Carries on the LME

Carries, which are comparable to "straddles" on the soft commodities markets, are put into effect by borrowing or lending. As their names suggest, these terms denote respectively buying cash or nearby and reselling forward, and the converse. In each case, both sides of the carry are done with the same counterparty, and the prices for both are agreed at the outset.

There is a difference here between a straightforward carry as outlined above and what is usually meant by a "spread" or a "straddle". In these latter, the intention is also to establish a market position – spot (cash) or nearby against futures – but the interposition of the clearing house makes transacting both legs of the deal with the same party impracticable. On the prompt, a seller tenders to, and a buyer takes up from, the clearing house. It is a technical difference only, but worth noting for all that.

Carries may conveniently be separated into three categories, each of which is motivated for different reasons. These reasons are (a) to prolong the life of a market position by rolling it forward, (b) as a financial operation in its own right, and (c) to square one's book in order, for example, to minimise interest costs on a temporarily long position. The first of these categories has been touched upon in the chapter on hedging, and it remains here only to consider certain matters of detail which can affect the financial if not the actual tonnage content of carries.

Rates for carries

For cash, and for each subsequent market day up to three months, two prices are or may be quoted, buyers' and sellers'. (There are not always two prices because it is not always certain that there would have been both bids and offers for every intervening market day. Where a price is required for a date, however, a Ring member will invariably oblige by offering to trade the date in question on the basis of buyers' and sellers' prices arrived at by extrapolation from those actually quoted for the nearest available dates.) There will always be a spread between buyers' and sellers' prices. The smallest will be equal to the minimum step in prices quoted in the Ring, namely £1 for tin, 50p for copper, aluminium and nickel, 25p for lead and zinc and 0.10p for silver. There are no maxima to spreads between buyers' and sellers' prices, and it often happens that under certain market conditions they can be quite wide, for example in a comparatively inactive market, or one tending at the time to be predominantly bullish or bearish.

In negotiating a carry on the LME, each party (be he borrower or lender) must first find a counterparty who is willing to trade for the dates required, and who will make a suitable price for doing so. It is here that "lender's rates" and "borrower's rates" come into play. Taking the following prices as an example:

cash buyers £675	3 months buyers £690
cash sellers £677	3 months sellers £692

a borrower would seek to buy at the lowest and sell at the highest; and if he were offering in the Ring he would endeavour to borrow from cash to three months at £17. In a contango, it is the lender who pays the contango and therefore in the same circumstances he would offer to lend from cash to three months at £13.

With a wide spread between buyers and sellers, and a small contango or backwardation ruling at the time, it could be that the difference between lender's and borrower's rates may be such as to extinguish altogether any purely financial advantage in a carry.

The "half and half" carry

The spread between lender's and borrower's rates has given rise to the use of half and half carries as a convenience by Ring members. Here, the difference may be split and each party to the transaction bears, or profits by, one half of that difference. Such a carry can be done only when there is an even number of warrants in the transaction, since one rate will apply to one half and the other rate to the second half of the total tonnage carried. In this way, one or more warrants will be traded at the borrower's rate and the same number at the lender's. A half and half carry is the only instance in Ring dealing where the minimum step in prices may be disregarded and a step of half that amount bid or offered. For purposes of accounting one half of the tonnage will be invoiced at one rate and the balance at the other so that effectively each has paid one half at the full rate.

When lending or borrowing in order to prolong the duration of a position on the Market it should be borne in mind that a change in the rate of the contango or backwardation will affect the costings of the second "leg" of the carry. This is a different situation from that obtaining in pricing further ahead than three months, and should be allowed for when hedging against such a long-term pricing arrangement. It is not in fact possible to prolong a "classic" hedge beyond the forward trading limit, except possibly in a continuing contango situation.

It has already been noted, but bears repetition, that a contango, being almost entirely comprised of money costs, can be projected forward in time beyond three months with passable accuracy. Assuming constant interest rates, it can be taken to widen as an arithmetical progression as it lengthens in time, and changes in rates can be taken into account should they occur. On the other hand, a backwardation is almost impossible to project with any degree of confidence; though as a generalisation it can be said that the back will tend to narrow towards really distant dates. It is also likely that even within the space of three months a back will be far from uniform, often deepening sharply over certain key dates which may be critical from the physical supply and demand standpoint.

Carries as an exercise in their own right
There could be said to be three main motives for carrying for purely financial reasons, of which the second and third are also related to the financial aspect of hedging. They are:

1. To profit by a ruling premium of forward over cash (the contango).
2. To minimise the adverse effects of, or maximise any potential bonus arising from, any change in contango or backwardation.
3. To transfer profits or losses from one accounting or fiscal period to another. (This is a highly specialised matter in which taxation looms as important if not more so than LME dealing. As such it is outside the scope of this study, and mentioned just in passing.)

Granted that there are usually a sufficient number who wish to lend or borrow – especially over short periods for book-squaring purposes and the like – there is rarely any difficulty in finding the other side to such an operation on the LME.

The first category embraces what the LME calls "contango financing" and is the equivalent of a "cash and carry" on the soft commodity markets. Here, a bank or other financial institution may make a legitimate profit by borrowing – buying cash and simultaneously selling forward – when the contango rate exceeds the net cost of money to itself. The contango reflects overall interest rates, and there are times when an institution or an individual has spare funds costing less than this. In such circumstances to buy cash and sell forward into the contango will lock in a profit equal to this difference. In doing this, the borrower has incidentally taken some of the inventory load off the market (or off stockholders with metal on warrant) in a surplus situation, as well as putting some kind of floor under cash prices which could well be sagging at such a time.

The second type of transaction might be done either as a variation of a straightforward financing transaction or as a fairly mild form of speculation. Having borrowed into a contango and established bought price for cash, for which the warrants are now held, and price due to be received on the future sale, the borrower might decide that prices had changed sufficiently for it to be opportune to sell his bought position for cash, take his profit (and probably save himself further interest on finance), and buy forward prompt the same date as he is due to deliver against his original borrow. If he is then buying into a reduced contango (and for less than the full three months) or even with a backwardation to assist him, this step too could show a marginal profit.

Variations on the theme are legion, and carries can be a fruitful source of profit with a reasonably limited risk, provided the operations are conducted astutely. They do, however, demand constant vigilance and attention to market movements, notably to changes in the relationship of cash to forward prices. Another factor to be taken into account is that of costs. Commissions on the LME are small, but a busy book in carries presupposes a large number of transactions. The incidence of even a small element of commission will therefore be heavier than it would in larger dealings with less jobbing in and out. A well-orientated member/client duo can, however, conduct an extremely profitable business in carries when markets are moving at all briskly.

Finally, some attention has to be given to borrowing and lending purely or mainly for the purpose of keeping a market book as nearly square as possible. This is of particular importance in times of rapidly moving prices and of course when interest rates are high. At such times, it can be expensive to be long of metal unnecessarily, and the cost of finance is appreciable even over an ordinary weekend if there is any significant tonnage being held. For this and for other reasons, a large proportion of a Ring member's daily activity is devoted to lending and borrowing across the Ring. Overnight carries are as a rule done "level": no rate will be charged and the operation will be regarded purely as a convenience. In other short-term carries, too, the price at which the metal was borrowed and lent need not actually change hands, the carrying rate only being transferred between the parties.

A further variation, and one very often carried out in the Ring between members, is to "borrow and lend-on" or vice versa. A member may offer, say, to borrow four warrants for 10 days from 3 March and lend-on. This means that he finds himself short on 3 March, long on 13 March and short again on 23 March. The transactions may be summarised as follows.

1. Member *A* buys four warrants from member *B*, prompt 3 March.
2. Member *A* delivers eight warrants to member *B* on 13 March.
3. Member *A* buys back four warrants from member *B* on 23 March.

In each case, the number of warrants transferred in transaction (2) is double that in (1) and (3), and all are carried out between the same two members.

The facility for trading in named dates makes such operations feasible, and in themselves they contribute very usefully to the extreme flexibility of LME dealings.

13
Options

Trading in options is a form of speculation in price movements with a limited risk. With an anticipated rise in, say, the price of copper, a speculator might go long, i.e. buy forward on the assumption that when he is due to take delivery in fulfilment of his forward purchase, the price will have so increased as to enable him to sell the position at a profit. Should he have divined wrongly, he stands to lose the difference between a high price paid for his forward purchase and a lower one realised on selling against it. This difference either way is never easily predictable at the time of the opening purchase. In order to limit his risk, therefore, the speculator might decide to purchase a *call option*. Here, he would pay a premium to the grantor of the option and on the prompt day he may either take it up (if prices have risen sufficiently) and sell against it or abandon the option having lost only the amount of the premium which was fixed and paid at the outset.

Risk on a short sale in anticipation of falling prices can be limited in a similar way by the purchase of a *put option* enabling the purchaser to sell to the grantor on prompt date at the basis price or striking price, which, like the amount of the premium, was established at the commencement.

An "each way" position can be taken with the purchase of a *double option* (put or call), usually at about double the premium. Just as the premiums required for put and call will not necessarily be the same (the amount of risk to the grantor in either case will of course differ according to conditions, as well as his own assessment of the risk of a movement unfavourable to him), so the overall premium on a double option will also reflect this difference.

In circumstances where the premium on a double option is less than twice that on "call" or "put" – due to one meriting at the time a higher premium than the other – it could be advantageous for the taker to purchase half the number of double options. One half of the double options may then be converted into calls or puts – depending on the market – and the whole "bundle" would therefore operate in the same direction. An example will show this.

Copper calls are available at £40 per tonne premium, but doubles at £70 per tonne only (not £80). Rather than buy, say, 100 tonnes of calls at £4000 total premium, the taker could buy 50 tonnes of doubles at £3750 total premium. He would then buy 50 tonnes forward in the market prompt the same date and at as near to the basis price as possible.

If prices rise, then the 50 tonnes of puts (the unprofitable side in this case) are covered by the 50 tonnes bought in the market. Should prices fall, then the 50 tonnes of puts will be used in order to close this bought position.

In this way, 50 tonnes of doubles have been converted into 100 tonnes of puts or calls – depending on price movements – at a saving of £250 in total premium.

As a rule, buying options will be a fruitful exercise in its own right only if prices are moving widely: the premium paid is irrecoverable, and therefore the price on the declaration day (when notice of the intention to exercise the option must be given) must have moved up or down by an amount larger than the premium plus commission and any interest incurred for an overall profit to be shown on the deal.

LME options are traded in the same contract lots, and for periods up to the same maximum forward dealing periods as are ordinary purchases and sales of warrants on the market. Individual arrangements as to longer periods may be made if the market justifies this, although they are always in months rather than in dates.

In outline, the procedure is for the purchaser ("taker") and the grantor of the option to fix the basis price at which the warrants will eventually change hands if the option is exercised. The premium is agreed and as a rule paid over to the grantor at the commencement. The amount of the premium in relation to the basis price will vary according to backwardation or contango rates ruling at the time, and the grantor's own assessment of likely market movements during the currency of the option. The grantor has to minimise the financial risk to himself, without the contrary risk of pricing himself out of the market.

The purchaser of the option must make his declaration (that he intends to take it up) in writing to the grantor before noon on the declaration day. This date will be set out in the contract, and as a rule on the LME it will fall on the same number of market days before prompt date as there are months in the total period of the option. Failure to make a formal (affirmative) declaration is taken automatically as abandonment of the option and consequent forefeiture of the premium.

At its simplest, therefore, purchase of a call option confers the right to buy (call for) the warrants on the prompt date at the basis price. If prices have risen over and above the cost of the premium plus incidentals, then a profit for the purchaser ("taker") ensues. If prices fall, or do not advance far enough, his only loss is the premium and these incidentals. The converse applies to a put option, which confers the right to sell to the grantor at the basis price.

Trading against options

To buy an option and then await results may often be frustrating, as prices see-saw or obstinately remain within too limited a bracket. It usually pays, therefore, to trade against options already bought.

Taking a call as an example, having bought one or more call options prompt three months (and it rarely repays the effort to trade only in singletons rather than multiples), the purchaser now has a position against which he can sell up to the same number of warrants without actually being caught short. He has bought the right to call for delivery of the warrants on the prompt date and so is in a position to sell (or, if the market is volatile, to job), in a like number of warrants.

This facility is of importance not only in producing a further marginal element of profit – effectively recouping some if not all of the premiums paid – but as a means of limiting potential loss of a more serious nature by actually converting a call into a put or vice versa. The taker of a call may very soon see that he has in fact bought his option at too high a price in the light of a downward trend now developing on the market, and that he is now therefore on what appears to be an automatic loser, unless there be a lucky reversal of the trend. He may take advantage of this movement, though, by selling short on the market against his options. Had the trend been in his favour at first, and then fallen away, and had he been astute enough to note this in time and make his short sale at or above the basis price of the options, then he would for practical purposes have converted a call into a put, and on a falling market.

146

Such active market dealing against established options can greatly increase their effectiveness, especially when prices are moving and there are appreciable short-term differences in contango or backwardation rates. It is absolutely necessary to ensure that the number of warrants traded against options never exceeds the number of the options themselves, lest an uncovered position arise.

As in any other form of forward dealing on the LME, a contango will militate in favour of a put – or sale on a future date – when it is likely that a purchase for cash or nearby against this sale can be made at an advantageous price. The converse in principle would apply to a backwardation, when the forward purchase (the call option) could in due course be liquidated by a sale for cash at a premium. However, a back usually implies unstable prices and may even presage a sharp fall (hence the saying "The bigger the back, the bigger the fall"), and by the prompt date the market might have declined sufficiently for the cash sale not to be profitable. Great vigilance, in whatever market operation is in train, is always essential when there is a backwardation ruling.

Granting options
This is a very specialised operation and the grantor must at all times see himself covered: both as to taking or making delivery should the option be exercised, and as to his ultimate position should it be abandoned. As a rule options will be exercised only if the price has moved in the taker's favour, and against the grantor, by at least the amount of the premium. To be fully covered the grantor of a call should be long at the right price in order to deliver against the call being exercised against him. But what if prices drift downwards? Here he must assume the role of psychologist and try to read the mind of the taker. If he exercises, all is well, but what if he should abandon? Our grantor is now long himself in a falling market. (The converse would have been the case had he granted a put.) And should prices indulge in what is graphically described as a "whipsaw", grey hairs are in store for the grantor of options without extremely strong backing.

Ideally, a grantor should have a position outside the market against which to sell options. He could, for example, make a stock of physical earn him the equivalent of a rate of interest if his options trading goes his way (he will have traded against them in the market), or he may – if they consist of registered brands – deliver ex-stock against a call or take into stock against a put, and average out the ensuing value of his stocks. Without such physical backing, the grantor should be sufficiently active as to be able to average the profit and loss on options he has sold. Obviously, for every loser there will not inevitably be a compensating winner in his hand, but there is some safety in numbers.

There are many professional grantors of options, but the practice is one to be viewed with great caution by any but a well-backed trader, who, preferably, has access to physical stocks.

Traded and dealer options

In an options transaction such as those which we have been considering there are two variables: premium and strike price. These are matters for agreement between grantor and taker, and because they are negotiable in this way it follows that any such option must remain a bilateral trade between these two parties. There is no "norm" against which a current option may be priced and sold or bought in open market. Two variations on the theme have been evolved, in order to make current options – those granted, and where declaration day has not yet arrived – more or less tradeable as such.

The first variation is the "dealer option". Here, the grantor offers options for sale at fixed strike prices for various periods and the only negotiable item, or variable, is the premium. Should the taker of such an option see premiums rising above that which he paid, he may offer it back to the grantor while it still has some time to run. He may take as his profit the difference between the original premium and whatever higher figure the grantor is now willing to offer for repurchase of the option. In dealer options the grantor is in fact "making a market" in premiums, and there are several members of the LME who make their own market thus in buying and selling dealer options.

The next step along this path, and one which is only recently attracting attention in the London commodity markets, is the organisation of an open and formalised market in buying and selling current options. These are known as "traded options", and with such a market a taker may re-sell not only to his original grantor but to any operator in the traded options market.

Strike prices are published for various maturity dates, and an open market in premiums ensues. The strike prices must, for obvious reasons, bear a definite relationship to going futures prices for the commodity but they do not necessarily vary from day to day in the same way. On a movement in market prices a new tranche of traded options is offered at a revised strike price.

When a taker realises that the going rate for premiums for a tranche of traded options is higher than that which he originally paid, he may offer his option in the market as an "in the money" option and take a profit rather than wait – with the attendant risk of a price reversal – until declaration day. Conversely, he may sell his option "out of the money" and so cut his potential loss since with lower premiums for a given strike price it follows that the trend is against the takers at that price.

There is a great deal of attraction in such a market, where the buying and selling of traded options becomes a business in its own right, and declarations and the exercise of the options the exception rather than the rule.

14
Pricing

There are two major sides to the pricing of metal on the LME: use of the official settlement price as the basis for purchases under a contract from a producer, and use of the market for the purpose of establishing, or protecting, a price for future deliveries or sales by dealing forward.

Contracts for physical material between producer and fabricator or importer: "back-pricing"
Unless there is a set producer price in operation, the vast majority of contracts for deliveries over a period are priced on the basis of the average LME settlement price during the month of shipment of each batch of material. Over the years, however, the tradition has emerged of producers allowing their larger customers – or those taking a fairly regular tonnage over each contract year – to price an agreed proportion of their intake against the LME settlement price announced the day previous to that on which a shipment is due for pricing on the terms of the contract. This facility is known as "pricing terms" or "back-pricing", and it is important in that it affords to the importer an opportunity to make a hedging profit as an offset against an adverse trend in the average prices, as well as to quote a firm price for a given day to any of his own customers. Under typical pricing terms an importer could secure to himself the option to price up to, say, 25% of his monthly intake on any one day, at the previous day's LME settlement price. There would additionally be a limit placed on the frequency of his exercising this

option within each month, for example not more than 50% of a month's total in any one week. (Under these particular terms, an importer could in fact price his whole month's intake "on the known" by pricing in two tranches in two successive weeks.)

In order to price thus, it is necessary that the instruction to do so is given before the commencement of official trading on the day of pricing. Once official trading has started, the previous day's settlement price has no further significance in this regard, and the importer must now wait until today's prices are announced, if he still wishes to price on the known.

Pricing terms are much valued by importers and fabricators: not least because they are thus themselves given a marked amount of latitude as to the actual sums they will pay over each month. They are also put in the position of being able to confer a similar privilege to certain of their own customers, and because of the way in which they facilitate hedging, the granting of such terms is an undoubted sales aid.

In a case where an importer has back-priced, say, 250 tonnes of his producer intake to yesterday's settlement price and then seen today's price come out at £10 per tonne higher, he has automatically won himself a bonus of £10 per tonne on a resale at today's price. To cover himself against a possible fall, however, it would be prudent for him to sell a like tonnage forward on the LME at the moment he books the 250 tonnes for his own intake. Thus:

10 June Settlement price £850. 3 months £830.
11 June at 11.00 a.m. importer advised that market appears to be rising, so books 250 tonnes at £850 (yesterday's settlement price) and sells 250 tonnes prompt 3 months on LME – now trading (11 June) at £835.
12 June Settlement price announced is £865 and 3 months is £835. Importer sells to customer at £865 (today's price) and buys in 3 months sale at £835.
Profit on physical is £15 per tonne, and zero on hedge.

If the market had turned after the back-pricing and hedge sale on 11 June, and settlement price come out at £840, with three months at £825, then the importer would lose £10 per tonne on his physical sale through having misread the market, but would recoup £10 per tonne on his hedge, thus safeguarding his overall position.

The whole system of back-pricing may appear to be one of the illogicalities in an otherwise mathematically logical marketing process. It was introduced at a time when the major primary producers were keen to tie their customers up to contracts extending over a period – usually one year at a time – and when prices were such that

151

some sort of sales aid was manifestly desirable in order to achieve this. After taking advantage of back-pricing terms, the larger importers were not slow in passing on a part of this advantage to their own customers; it would now be hard to see the system readily abandoned after having become to some extent hallowed by tradition.

Other aspects of using the LME as a medium for establishing a price have been touched on in the chapter on hedging, but there remain some further examples which are worth a little attention.

Pricing in advance of delivery
It frequently happens that material must not only be ordered but also priced some time before delivery. (This is different from pricing on an unknown settlement price on date of delivery, which has already been noted.) Terms for pricing in advance of delivery vary from case to case, but two that are fairly typical are the option to price on the known settlement price at the date of placing the order, or to price on an as yet unknown settlement price at an agreed date between placing the order and delivery of the material.

In the first instance, the purchaser would book for delivery, say, three months hence at the known LME settlement price of the day previous, thus establishing a firm price for the material from the outset. He may, however, be selling his own product based on LME prices current at the time of such sale. He must therefore cover himself against a possible fall in prices between now and the date of delivery of physical to him, and pricing the material to be contained in his own product. This he would do by selling a like tonnage on the LME prompt the date of delivery of the physical. A fall in market values will enable the purchaser to recover the difference when he closes this short hedge, and cost his own sales on the basis of the later LME prices ruling at time of these sales. On a rising market, he would lose on the hedge but recover on sale to his own customers, based on the ensuing higher price.

Conversely, should the purchaser price on an unknown LME settlement price midway (say) between order and delivery, yet be required to give a firm price as of now for his own future sale, he would execute a buying or long hedge. Here, he would price his own sales on whatever figure he was able to buy forward at in the market, prompt the date agreed for pricing the physical delivery to him.

By using the LME thus, the purchaser has been able in the first instance to cover himself against risks on pricing his intake now, and pricing his products in the future. In the second instance he has established a firm price for the finished product now, despite uncertainty as to the eventual cost to him of the metal to be incorporated in it.

Variations on the theme are legion, but the basic principle of covering on the market remains valid. Further complications are introduced when there are options to price on either cash or forward prices: here contango and backwardation must be allowed for, and the principle observed that buying forward into a back and selling into a contango are the more profitable options.

Example
Pricing on unknown 6 weeks forward for delivery 3 months forward, and making firm quote to own customer *now* on a sale due 3 months forward.

Date	LME official prices	Operations with supplier	Operations on LME	Operations with customer
15 March	Cash – £880.	Orders metal for delivery on 16 June – to be priced on LME cash quote on 30 April.	Buys forward, prompt 30 April at £865.	Quotes him a firm price of £865 for delivery 16 June.
	3 months ·£850.			
30 April	Cash – £920.	Prices intake at £920.	Sells cash at £920 – closing his forward bought position (at £865).	
16 June	Prices are are now immaterial.	Intake delivered, and paid for at £920.		Sells to his customer at £865.

(a) Bought metal from supplier at £920 – a notional loss of £40 per tonne between LME cash price on day of *ordering* (15 March) and day of *pricing* (30 April).
(b) Made profit (real) of £55 per tonne on his LME operation. Thus his actual net cost was £865, being the £920 paid to his supplier *minus* the £55 profit on the LME hedge.

He may now calculate his own costs and margin on the operation, having safeguarded himself from any uncertainty as to price of the material.

15
Settlement Price

As the settlement price forms the basis for all transactions carried out on the LME, as well as for pricing a very high proportion of direct producer to consumer trade, some words of explanation and enlargement are called for. In so far as direct dealings are concerned, a producer in one country who sells ores or metal to a consumer in another must have some point of reference upon which a mutually acceptable price can be established. The daily LME settlement price forms such a datum; each party to a direct over-the-frontier deal may base his own calculations on this known (and published) factor.

The LME prices are announced after the close of official trading on every market day; and this announcement includes the settlement price, which in point of fact is the same as the cash sellers' price on the day. It has a double significance. Outside the LME, settlement price is taken as the reference for contracts based on LME quotations and now due for pricing. It is also taken as that day's component in any arrangements for pricing on the average of LME quotations over a prearranged period of time. Thus, the settlement price is very widely accepted as the base price for sales of physical metal which are not actually done on the Market at all.

Deals which have been done on LME contracts, and which are now prompt, are all concluded at settlement price. Difference either way between this figure and the individual contract prices – perhaps negotiated as long as three months beforehand – are then calculated and shown separately in the account.

A typical LME Ring member's account to a client might look as follows:

Brand	Pieces	Weight (tonnes)	Rent		
XYZ	220	25,034	24/9/82	1 week	
XYZ	221	24,999	24/9/82	1 week	
		50,033		2 weeks	
	At £428 per tonne in warehouse London				£21,414.12
	Less Rent at 12p per tonne per week				6.00
					£21,408.12

Contract price £431 per tonne
Settlement price £428 per tonne
    Difference £3 per tonne   150.00

                                                                 £21,558.12

Although this method appears unnecessarily complicated at first sight, it is logical in that the difference between present prices and original contract prices is at once apparent. Anyone who has taken the step of buying or selling forward will have an interest in this difference (hedging, profit-taking, etc.). It also makes far easier the handling of contracts between Ring members which have been cancelled out as to actual delivery by execution of counter-contracts for identical tonnages and prompt date.

If these contracts were entered into at different times in the 3-month period before the prompt date (and in all probability with different counterparties as well), it follows that they will have been made at differing prices. If member A had bought 100 tonnes for 20 June from member B on 21 April and then sold 100 tonnes for 20 June to member C on 15 May, there would be little point in his collecting the warrants from B and paying him for them, and straightaway handing them on to C and collecting from him.

The LME "clearing" here comes into play as a method of dealing each day with deliveries between Ring members in respect of all contracts now prompt. The notion of the clearing originated as long ago as 1890, and the form in use up to the present was the brainchild of the ingenious Mr Neems, a Committee member, in 1909. It is perhaps best described by way of example, showing how the movement both of large sums of money and of valuable warehouse warrants may be reduced to a minimum. The saving in time, cost and the risk of misplacement of documents of title is obvious.

Before 6 p.m. on each market day every Ring member must provide the LME Office with a clearing form in respect of each metal: showing tonnages to be delivered to, or taken up from, each other Ring member with whom he has contracts prompt the day following. At the foot of the forms he indicates the overall total he is due to take up or deliver. Note that no mention of prices is made on these forms. The staff in the office collate the returns early the following morning and direct members due overall to deliver to make their deliveries to those due overall to receive. In this way it is possible – indeed almost certain – that a Ring member will transfer warrants to or from another with whom in fact he had not done any business for that particular prompt. It has simply happened that the one is due overall to deliver and the other to receive: their own original counterparties having in the interim closed out their positions by buying or selling for that date.

All transfers of warrants under directions of the clearing are effected at the previous day's settlement price. Differences between this and individual contract prices are then dealt with separately, and directly between the parties concerned without intervention by the clearing. The effect of this procedure is for the first seller in any chain of deals to deliver warrants to the last buyer at the settlement price, whilst all in the chain settle between themselves as to any difference between this amount and their own contracted prices.

The essential distinction between this "clearing" and a full clearing house is that at no time is anyone's contractual obligation shifted on to anyone else. Individual contracts stand as such for the various prompt dates – there is no provision for early "washing-out" – and differences between settlement price and contract prices remain the responsibility of the members concerned as and when they arise.

Example

In one 3-month period:

    A sold to B 100 tonnes @ £600 per tonne = £60,000
    B sold to C 50 tonnes @ £620 per tonne = £31,000
    B sold to D 50 tonnes @ £650 per tonne = £32,500
    D sold to A 50 tonnes @ £660 per tonne = £33,000

Therefore on prompt date:

    A is a net seller of 50 tonnes
    B is square as to tonnage bought and sold
    C is a net buyer of 50 tonnes
    D is square as to tonnage bought and sold

On prompt date, the settlement price (SP) is £700 per tonne.

156

A delivers 50 tonnes to C and receives £35,000 = 50 × £700 SP

receives difference from D of   2,000 = between contract price £660
700 × 50 tonnes.

37,000

He pays difference to B of   10,000 = between contract price £600
and SP £700 × 100 tonnes.

He gets net   £27,000 = proceeds of 100 tonnes sold
@ £600,
less cost of 50 bought @ £660.

B No delivery or take-up of warrants
He receives difference from A of £10,000 = see above
He pays difference to C of   4,000 = between contract price £620
and SP £700 × 50 tonnes.
He pays difference to D of   2,500 = between contract price £650
and SP £700 × 50 tonnes.
He gets net   £ 3,500 = proceeds of 50 tonnes sold
@ £620 and 50 at £650 less cost
of 100 bought at £600.

C No delivery of warrants, but takes up 50 tonnes from A
He receives difference from B of   4,000 = see above
He pays A   35,000 = 50 tonnes at £700 SP

He pays out net   £31,000 = cost of 50 tonnes at £620.

D No delivery or take up of warrants
He receives difference from B of   £ 2,500 = see above
He pays difference to A of   2,000 = see above

He gets net   £   500 = after purchase at £32,500
and sale at £33,000.

The procedure as a rule works well enough, and undoubtedly saves time and expense. However, difficulties can occur if, for example, a member takes up warrants via the clearing where there may be a defect as to title, or as to quality or quantity of metal covered by those warrants. In such a case, he may have taken them (on instructions from the clearing) from another member with whom he was not in a contractual situation and therefore to whom he has no recourse should there be any such defect. The rarity of such contretemps does not entirely outweigh the disadvantages of the system in this respect, and there is a strong school of thought that warrants ought to be delivered to and collected from a central "pool" with its own insurance arrangements.

A further point to note is that while trading on the LME is done "on the round tonnage", i.e. the precise 25 tonne warrant for, say, copper, there is a permitted tolerance of up to 2% plus or minus in the actual weight of metal making up any one warrant. When warrants are delivered and priced on the basis of the round tonnage any such incidental over- or underweight within the permitted tolerance is accounted for at the previous day's settlement price. There is scope afforded here for a certain amount of selectivity by the seller in delivering warrants, since he already knows the price at which the over- or underweight may be invoiced and by the time he must proffer the warrant he is also aware of the latest trend in prices.

PART FOUR
The Outlook

16
Outside Influences

Value added tax

The prospect of value added tax being introduced in the United Kingdom in 1973 was viewed by all the London commodity markets with some justifiable apprehension. With the facilities offered by the markets for buying and selling for future delivery and with the more or less complete unpredictability of the prices at which forward contracts would be settled, the problems appeared to be insoluble. From the practical standpoint too the sheer weight of numbers of transactions (many involving the same parcel of merchandise as it was traded on the market prior to a future delivery) would bring in its train an intolerable accounting burden. Furthermore, anomalies would inevitably arise if tax were to be accounted for at the same rate and at the same time on a market transaction – closing a hedge for example – and on the physical side of the hedge, which could have been contracted at a quite different price.

The problem was basically to ensure that both physical and market sides of hedging and comparable transactions were taxed on the same footing, whilst at the same time ensuring freedom from tax accounting for all the myriad market deals. The exemption from VAT of any transaction or class of person, far from solving this problem, simply makes it the more fractious.

VAT is in essence a turnover tax with provision for deducting sums already paid to suppliers in the course of business ("inputs") from tax now due to be remitted to the authorities from payments of VAT received from customers in response to one's own invoices

161

("outputs"). Each registered trader collects tax from his purchasers, deducts whatever he may himself have paid to his own suppliers, and accounts for the difference with the authorities.

The ultimate purchaser for consumption (retail) not being registered pays VAT and may not reclaim this. Thus, your inputs are your outgoings, your outputs are your income, if you are registered for VAT you do not pay it (you pass it on) and if you are unregistered you do pay it.

The scheme ultimately adopted for the commodity markets by agreement with HM Customs and Excise – the authority in the UK responsible for VAT – was made possible by the recognition in Britain of VAT at "zero rate". This is absolutely logical, and simply means that tax is chargeable, but at 0%. Under such a category, it is possible for a trader to reclaim or set off any VAT paid by him as inputs in his own settlements of his own suppliers' invoices, yet at the same time not to invoice his own customers for VAT – save at 0%. If he has a net credit balance of inputs over outputs at the end of each accounting period (usually three months), he may reclaim direct from the authorities.

Having agreed the principle on which any such scheme might rest (and granted zero rating to make it possible at all), it remained only to delineate the actual limits of the concept of each market – within which it would be permissible to trade all contracts at zero VAT. Note how essential is the distinction between "zero VAT" and "no VAT at all" – the interposition of a VAT-exempt stage in a series of transactions has the effect of causing the transaction immediately preceding it to be taxed twice over. Here, the representatives of the markets and of HM Customs maintained long and detailed discussions, and in the event a remarkably simple basic pattern was arrived at.

Material being brought into a market must be so brought with VAT accounted for. Material being sold out of the market must similarly be sold with VAT accounted for at the price at which that sale is made. Material being bought and sold within the market may be traded at zero rate VAT. Thus, there is no accounting problem in dealing with VAT on very numerous purely market deals (carries, etc.), whilst at the same time inputs (costs) may be allowed for VAT in market hedging deals in just the same way as are allowed on their physical counterparts.

The VAT system for the commodity markets was set out in the Terminal Markets Order of 1973, and this has subsequently been amended so as to include new markets as they are admitted within the scope of the Order.

Essentially, once metal has been placed on warrant and VAT accounted for, all further dealings in that metal where there is no delivery out of warehouse and where at least one of the parties is an LME member are zero rated for VAT. The zero rating extends to actual deliveries in dealings where both parties are members. On a physical delivery to a non-member, he must account for VAT (against a VAT invoice raised by the selling member) at the price at which he bought the metal.

From the foregoing it can be seen that a non-member buying a warrant from a member may sell it back to a member without paying VAT on either transaction. But sale of the warrant by him to another non-member is subject to VAT, whether there be physical delivery or not.

Unfortunately, it was not possible to include rents charged by UK warehouses within the scope of the Order and these therefore are subject to VAT against an invoice raised by warehouse.

The position of any user of the LME as regards his other taxation, be it personal income tax or some form of tax on the profits of a company or partnership, is very much a matter of individual circumstances. In fact, the taxation position of commodity market dealings is a large and complicated subject in its own right, and as such must remain outside the scope of this study. If a general principle may be stated, it is that profits arising out of any commodity market dealings are as a rule looked at by the Inland Revenue as trading profits and are taxable as such.

The EEC

As we have noted when considering individually the metals traded on the LME, the EEC does exercise a measure of fiscal protection in respect of those – notably aluminium, lead and zinc – where there is an appreciable volume of production within the Community. Since the United Kingdom became a member, there has been a fairly protracted process of "harmonisation" to deal with both EEC duties and tariffs and with the remaining vestiges of the old Empire Preference. The problem-child now remaining is the heavy *ad valorem* duty on aluminium imported into the EEC.

There are also various differences on the treatment of metal in store. Some delivery points are regarded as being outside the Community for customs purposes, entailing the full export and

163

re-import formalities for metal deposited there and later taken up for use within the EEC. Others are regarded as being within the Community, and still others as being "transit" warehouses where there are no financial or documentary problems as to the movement of metal in or out. To all concerned with the physical side of metals trading, our only advice on this rather knotty subject would be to consult a member or the Secretary of the LME for advice and up-to-date information.

Exchange control

All restrictions were of course removed in the United Kingdom in 1979. However, since there must remain the possibility – if no more – of the re-imposition of controls, a brief review of how they operated when last imposed may be of interest – let us hope, of academic interest only!

On the re-opening of the commodity markets after the Second World War, the Bank of England as the administrator of exchange control regulations set up a "scheme" for each commodity. LME members were admitted as participants in the metals scheme on the recommendation of the Committee, and undertook to furnish the Bank with confidential returns of their own and their clients' positions at regular intervals. In return, they were freed from some of the more irksome restrictions, especially in respect of dealings in metal warehoused outside the sterling area. Payment in such cases could be made in sterling to an external account, or in foreign currency. Non-resident clients of members were called upon to confirm in writing (as a part of their contract) that they would stand bound by the provisions of the scheme.

A pleasant by-product of the system was the quarterly Liaison Committee meetings held at the Bank between its officials and representatives of the LME. Apart from the business directly in hand, much other useful ground was covered in these semi-formal discussions.

17

LME quo vadis?

We have now examined the manner in which the LME goes about its business, and have given some consideration to what we have called its philosophy. Since the latter must to a great extent govern the former, what changes in outlook and principle may be foreseen? At this juncture, it can be said that signs of any significant shift in either – or in overall policy – are few. This is not by any means a symptom of ossification, nor of the governing bodies of the LME resting on their laurels with a perfect market under their care. Those who are in command of these matters are as alive as anyone to the manifold and changing forces that influence such an entity as the LME. Indeed, without such awareness they would hardly be suited to the commodity futures business where adaptability – and a dash of opportunism – are essential qualifications.

Rather, the cause of what at first sight may look like obsessive conservatism lies in experience gained from the LME's occasional forays into other fields, or experiments with other methods of trading. As early as the 1960s a proposal was put forward for a cleared market in silver, and in 1973–74 a lengthy study into a mutual guarantee corporation along US lines was undertaken. That neither to date has come any closer to fruition, taken with the continuing success of the silver market on the LME (despite the hectic days of the Silver Bulls) and the continuing financial stability of the LME membership as a whole, indicates that, in the light of experience to date, neither has proven necessary. Both are, arguably, desirable and could of themselves afford comfort by their very existence. But both would by their introduction presuppose a radical change in LME thinking.

As to the likelihood of its association with the gold futures market moving the LME any nearer to adopting the practices of other exchanges, the reverse – if initial experience gives any sign – is more likely the case. Certain of what might be regarded as by-products of such a system do, however, have a relevance. With a clearing house, for example, "marking to market" or the strict application of variation margins in line with daily price fluctuations is essential. So also is the need to register all trades between clearing house members, with its consequential deterrence of off-market trading between them. The increasing concern with the protection of the outside client which is being expressed, and which is evidenced in Professor Gower's study and what may follow from it, inevitably brings both of these requirements to the forefront. Whilst a clearing house member deals with his non-member clients as a principal to a non-transferable contract, the fact that in his in-market dealings he is himself marked to market makes it very hard for him not to mete out the same treatment to the whole corpus of his own clients.

It could well be, therefore, that a more rigid, or even an ordained, system for calling variation margins may be imposed upon LME trading. It could also be that the present highly active interdealer (off-market) trading may have to be curtailed, if only to ensure the recording of trades in order to facilitate calling margins to the satisfaction of the overall "monitor", whoever he may be.

With the withdrawal of exchange control, the watchdog function of the Bank of England was altered, to become a looser and altogether less formal affair. This is by no means an unmixed blessing in the eyes of the Exchange since the Bank, by its very closeness to the markets, became something of a protagonist for them in their dealings with other authorities. Today the markets find themselves very much more on their own in this regard. One effect on them all – including the LME despite its long tradition of independence of thought and action – has been to draw them closer together for mutual protection from the "hosts of Midian" in the persons of those in authority in other areas, which now include the Commission of the EEC.

So far any such drawing together has been somewhat hesitant, consisting in the main of the creation *ad hoc* of committees to consider individual matters ("threats" would be too strong a word). Whether the trend will develop further and whether the LME will follow it or remain outside any resultant pan-market groupings remains to be seen. It should be borne in mind, however, that the LME is itself an exchange covering (at present) seven different materials and with an active interest in an eighth; of the other exchanges, apart from LIFFE, probably only the IPE seems likely to follow this multi-commodity pattern.

On more technical matters the extension of the number and spread of the LME delivery points would seem to have progressed as far as is likely in the foreseeable future. The basic arguments remain the same, that a large number of delivery points may assist a hedging market and can be a positive benefit to consumers in areas near to them. (Producers are often chary of turning their output loose to such an extent, with inevitable diminution of any influence over its whereabouts at any time, or its ultimate destination.) Paradoxically, though, it is probably the fact that in LME trading an appreciable proportion of contracts do actually run to maturity and result in physical movement of metal out of warehouse and into use which inhibits the proliferation of delivery points. This is another factor distinguishing the LME from pure futures markets in other commodities, the outcome no doubt of the LME's origin as a trading forum for merchants in physicals. Difficulties for consumers can arise when warrants in far-away places are tendered on the prompt date, which on balance may outweigh advantages to "local" consumers.

The establishment of viable exchanges in other areas using a form of warrant compatible with those in use on the LME could, on the other hand, lead to an organised secondary market in the transfer of, and arbitrage in, such warrants. Meantime, it would appear that Western European points are adequate from the point of view of both number and distribution to meet the sometimes conflicting requirements of the hedger seeking a liquid market and the buyer requiring the physical delivery of the metal. A further point to consider in this context is that the banks and other financial institutions who "borrow" warrants themselves for purposes of contango-financing, and who provide finance to others on the security of LME warrants, might look askance at paper covering remotely located metal as collateral for such finance.

As to any immediate extension of the number of metals traded, this is less than likely in the near future, unless the need were suddenly to arise. (The LME is as quick as any other exchange to recognise and seize an opportunity.) Aluminium and nickel are

167

both historically recent introductions and, although it is not traded in the Ring, gold is still to a great extent in its infancy as a London market in futures. There has to be a time for assimilation.

Perhaps a more likely development will be an extension, and formalisation, of LME options trading. We have already seen how a traded options market operates – such a market in the soft commodities is certain to appear before long – and traded options in metals would have undoubted attractions to trade grantors and to non-trade takers alike. But this development too may presuppose some form of the clearing, or at the least the recording, of dealings.

In its attitude to membership the LME remains steadfast, and an active association with trading physicals is now probably even more essential to any applicant for membership than it has been in the recent past. This is no bad thing. Perpetuation of its "by the trade and for the trade" tradition must remain the LME's strong suit in the shifting pattern of external influence, and occasional attempts at interference, at both domestic and international level. If the Exchange has come a long way from the informal gatherings of London merchants to the discipline of an international market with a high degree of self-regulation of its practices and procedures, its way has been a consistent one and it has not lost sight of its aims.

Appendix 1
Glossary

Arbitrage: Dealings whose profitability depends on the difference in price between one market and another, or between one currency value and another. Typical LME examples would be buying copper or silver in London on the LME and offering in New York on the New York Commodity Exchange (Comex). Dealings in silver may also be arbitraged between the LME and the bullion market.

Arbitration: All LME contracts, as well as many contracts for metals not necessarily traded on the LME, provide for any dispute arising to be settled by the appointment of two or occasionally three arbitrators. A decision by the arbitrators is essential before any dispute may be taken to court. The English courts are supportive of arbitration in commercial disputes and would be unlikely to allow a case arising from an LME dispute to proceed where arbitration had not first been resorted to.

Assay: Analysis of metals submitted in order to arrive at confirmation of their purity. May be done by any of several methods (spectroscopy, etc.) and produces a list of other elements found in the sample, and their percentage of the whole.

ASTM: The American Society for Testing Materials. The official body in the USA for laying down standards as to purity as well as methods to be adopted for sampling and assaying.

169

Authorised clerk: Anyone admitted as such on the LME and thereby authorised to deal in the Ring on behalf of his employer. The status is purely an LME one, and the individual's status in his own organisation is for this purpose irrelevant.

Back-pricing (*see also* Pricing terms): A regular customer of a smelter or refiner or other supplier may be permitted to price a proportion of his month's intake on the known LME settlement price quoted the day previous to the date of pricing the intake. The proportion to be so priced is laid down in the contract, and the consumer – if he wishes to avail himself of the facility – must place his order before commencement of official trading on the LME on the date in question.

Backwardation (often abbreviated to "Back"): Denotes the premium of cash or nearby dates over three months or remote dates. There is no limit to a backwardation.

There is a theory that when the market is in equilibrium as to supply and demand, a backwardation is a logical state of affairs: since producers selling forward in order to hedge their own anticipated supplies to the market will expect to pay a premium in order to do so. Consumer hedging will, of course, work in the opposite direction. None the less, it is probably true that in "ideal" conditions as to supply and demand a modest backwardation should be expected.

N.B. Both Backwardation and Contango (*q.v.*) may show peaks or troughs for various dates within the forward trading period for which they are expressed. They do not necessarily progress in a straight line from cash to three months.

Bear: One who anticipates a fall in market values.

Borrowing: Buying cash or a nearby date and re-selling further forward. Both transactions are done at the same time and with the same counterparty, at prices and for dates agreed at the outset. A borrower pays a premium if he borrows into a backwardation, and receives a premium should he borrow into a contango.

BSI: The British Standards Institute. The official body in the United Kingdom for laying down standards as to purity as well as methods for sampling and assaying metals.

170

Brand: All metals deliverable on the LME must be of a brand registered as "good delivery" by the Committee. Brands, of which there may be many produced to different specifications and of different qualities by any given smelter or refiner, are as a rule identifiable by some distinguishing mark.

Bull: One who anticipates a rise in market values.

Buyer over: A bidder who is still unsatisfied (i.e. still calling his bid) at the close of a Ring. An unsatisfied buyer. If he is the latter, then his bid will be the official buyers' price for the day, in the second Ring.

Carries: The generic term for borrowing and lending, or a combination of the two. A carry may be extended for up to two weeks beyond the three months' time limit applied to buying and selling operations.

A carry is frequently used in order to roll a buying or selling trade forward in time, rather than take (or make) delivery on the original prompt date, or close-out by executing a trade in the contrary sense. It is essentially an exercise in fluidity, since changing contango or backwardation rates will apply.

Cash: A contract on the LME for settlement and for delivery (of warrants) on the day following.

Cash today: A contract between Ring members for settlement the same day. This must be done before 12.30 p.m. on the day in question.

Clearing (not to be confused with a Clearing house (q.v.)): The market mechanism whereby sellers overall deliver to buyers overall at the ruling settlement price. *See* Settlement price for detailed explanation.

Clearing house: May be either an independent body, or one owned by members of the market in question. A clearing house registers all contracts done in the market, and may substitute one party for another by novation. Thus, if a trader has both bought and sold the same number of lots for the same delivery month (not trading days as on the LME), he may drop out of the transaction as the clearing house matches his original counterparties with each other.

171

The clearing house also guarantees fulfilment of every contract registered; and as a safeguard calls for an initial deposit (fixed throughout life of contract) and further margins from those with open contracts where prices are moving against them. Favourable price movements could give rise to a return of margins, but in practice those doing a large or regular turnover tend to have a regular credit line with the clearing house for this purpose, supported by guarantees or by collateral.

Closing out: Execution of a contract for a date and tonnage which will cancel a previous obligation by matching it as to date and tonnage (though not price, where difference is treated as the profit element on the deal). On the LME it is necessary to await the prompt date before closing out, whereas with a Clearing house (q.v.) it may be done when the second contract is entered into.

Commission house: An institution, often of international coverage, which places orders with members of the exchanges on behalf of its own clients. Clients' individual purchase and sale orders may be aggregated, and form part of larger orders which the commission house then places in its own name. Several commission houses are members of the LME.

Consumer (*see also* Fabricator): Any organisation taking in bar, slab or ingot as traded on the LME and converting it to other forms of finished or semi-finished products. Not to be confused with one who buys and may hold warehouse warrants but never actually takes up the metal for use.

Contango: The premium commanded by three months or remote dates over cash or nearby dates. It expresses the costs of carrying metal over the period and therefore has a definite limit; i.e. money costs plus warehouse rent plus insurance.

Contract price: The price agreed between the parties at which an LME contract is entered into. Margin on Prompt date (q.v.) between this figure and the official Settlement price (q.v.) is the market Difference (q.v.).

Contract weight: The LME contracts provide for delivery of set amounts (25 tonnes for copper, lead, zinc and aluminium; 6 tonnes for nickel; 5 tonnes for tin; 10,000 troy ounces for silver). There is a clause in the contracts which allows up to 2% either side of the exact contract weight as good delivery.

Custom smelter: An organisation refining into bar, slab or ingot from materials (e.g. blister copper, scrap, concentrates, etc.) provided by others who then take back the refined shapes. The custom smelter derives his profit from the "returning charge" on these activities.

Delivery point: A location (usually a port) approved as such by the Board of the Company, on recommendation by the Committee, within which one or more registered warehouses are located. Many factors – geographical, economic, etc. – may determine the choice of a delivery point which, therefore, becomes a matter of LME policy, hence sanctioned by both Board and Committee.

Difference: Trades are done between the parties at the agreed contract price. Deliveries of warrants in respect of trades done are effected at the settlement price ruling on the prompt date of such delivery. Margin (if any) between settlement price and the original contract price is a difference and is accounted for separately.

Trades closed out before prompt date and which do not result in any transfer of warrants will as a rule result in a difference: the margin of profit to one party or the other.

Execution: Under the LME principal's contract, a Ring member may deal with a client at a price agreed between them, specified by the client or left in any of several ways to the discretion of the member. In the event that the member is not able to obtain the exact price in the Ring for the date and tonnage in question, he may none the less execute with the client at the agreed price, and bear any difference himself.

Fabricator (or sometimes "Semi-fabricator"): A Consumer (*q.v.*) who is in business to convert bar, slab, ingot or cathode, etc., into finished products or into semi-fabrications such as rod, extrusions, angle or tube.

Hedging: Covering a forward commitment in physical metal by entering into an equal and opposite commitment (in terms of tonnage and prompt date) on the market. Loss on the one will be equated by profit on the other.

173

Interoffice or interdealer trading: Name loosely given to bids and offers between Ring members made on the telephone each day outside official Ring trading. Whilst this period undoubtedly affords Ring members an opportunity to "test the market", it has possibly an opposite effect in that such trading is not done in the full publicity of Ring dealings.

Kerb trading: Dealings in the Ring or in the Room, and therefore done in the open market, between Ring members, yet outside official or the afternoon "unofficial" but still formalised market.

Kerb dealings have significance in that they enable a Ring member perhaps to complete business either interrupted by the Bell in official trading or which might have been too large in volume for a particular official market to have contained without an effect on prices. They are also a very large part of the essential flexibility of the LME in that they provide the time, opportunity and market for the multiplicity of book-squaring transactions which ought to be done before a day's business is closed.

Lending: Selling cash or a nearby date and repurchasing three months or at a remoter date. The converse of Borrowing (*q.v.*).

Lifting a leg: Closing-out one half of a back-to-back deal such as a lending or borrowing. The trader is now uncovered to the extent of the remaining (open) commitment.

Long (Going long): Buying forward on the market, and thus being "long" of metal for a given date. May be a speculative position in anticipation of rising prices when the bought position may be closed-out by selling advantageously, or may be a market position taken against a contrary physical commitment.

Options: These make it possible, on payment of a premium, to buy (call) or sell (put) on the declaration day at the basis or striking price agreed when the option was taken out, or to abandon the option on forfeit of the premium only should the market not respond to the forecast of the taker of the option. In this way, potential losses on an adverse price movement may be limited to the amount of the premium.

Pre-market: Dealings between Ring members (and between Ring members and their clients) done largely by telephone before official trading commences. An important part of member-to-client dealings will be on account of clients exercising back-pricing facilities.

The confidentiality of such dealings may, it is argued, militate against the sort of full disclosure which would otherwise have facilitated pricing in the open (official or kerb) market.

Pricing: Using the official LME price (or a formula based on the average of such prices over a period) as the basis for purchase price of physical metal.

Pricing terms: *See* Back-pricing.

Producer: May refer to a miner, i.e. producer of ores or concentrates, or to a refiner of these into ingot or other merchantable form. In this latter sense it also covers converters of scrap into secondary metal.

Prompt date: The date (always a working day) on which a forward LME contract becomes due for settlement.

Seller over: An offeror who is still offering at the close of a Ring. (*See* Buyer over.)

Semi-fabricator: A producer of semis (or semi-finished products).

Semis: Metal which has been fashioned into any of a number of recognised shapes such as tube, angle, etc.

Settlement price: The official cash seller's price at the close of the second Ring of official trading. Is used as the basis for trades in physical metal done outside the LME, as well as for internal accounting purposes on all LME trades now prompt for settlement. (In such cases, the difference between the settlement price on prompt date and the original contract price is separately accounted.)

Short: Sold forward. The converse of Long or Going long (*q.v.*).

Stocks: Metal on warrant in a registered LME warehouse. LME stocks (of which the total amount is published weekly) are *not* the property of the Exchange, but of the holders of the warrants at the time.

Stop loss: A buying or selling order placed in advance, which has the effect of cancelling out a previously contracted selling or buying order (the two are indeed often placed at the same time).

Warehouse: Any location having covered storage, with adequate security provided, which has been inspected and approved by the LME for registration as an approved warehouse. Warehouses may be in several categories, e.g. *free-port* or "outside customs territory"; *bonded* or "within customs territory" yet able to hold goods on which import duty or import-VAT have not yet been levied; *transit,* which is comparable to bonded; or *inland,* where duty, etc., has been paid on goods stored.

Warrant: Document of title issued by warehouse conferring title to set parcel of goods (*see* LME warrant weights) to person named on face of the document. Warrant may at any time be endorsed to another nominee or to "bearer", making it a readily negotiable document from the standpoint of its use as collateral for bank finance, etc. Warrants are the accepted documents on the LME and as such may change hands rapidly during trading on the market, secure in the knowledge that the underlying security (the metal) lies in warehouse and available to the current holder of a warrant.

White contract: Name given to contracts between LME Ring members and clients in respect of physical metal for forward delivery, frequently over periods extending well beyond the three months life of the standard LME contracts.

Appendix 2
Ring Trading Times

A. Official

11.45–11.50	Options (in all metals)
11.50–11.55	Silver
11.55–12.00	Aluminium
12.00–12.05	Copper
12.05–12.10	Tin
12.10–12.15	Lead
12.15–12.20	Zinc
12.20–12.25	Nickel
12.25–12.30	Interval
12.30–12.35	Copper higher grade
12.35–12.40	Copper standard cathodes
12.40–12.45	Tin
12.45–12.50	Lead
12.50–12.55	Zinc
12.55–13.00	Aluminium
13.00–13.05	Nickel
13.05–13.10	Silver

Official prices for the day are quoted after the last of the above Rings.

B. Unofficial

15.25–15.30	Lead
15.30–15.35	Zinc
15.35–15.40	Copper
15.40–15.45	Tin
15.45–15.50	Aluminium/Nickel
15.50–15.55	Silver
15.55–16.00	Interval
16.00–16.05	Lead
16.05–16.10	Zinc
16.10–16.15	Copper higher grade
16.15–16.20	Copper standard cathodes
16.20–16.25	Tin
16.25–16.30	Aluminium
16.30–16.35	Nickel
16.35–16.40	Silver

Appendix 3
LME Registered Brands

COPPER BRANDS

Official list issued by the Committee of the London Metal Exchange of the brands and descriptions deliverable in fulfilment of contracts for Copper.

Higher grade: wirebars
Electrolytic copper in the form of wirebars of standard dimensions in the weight range of 90 kg to 125 kg.

Australia	Erands—ISA
Belgium	UMK—UMK O
Canada	CCR—ORC
Chile	AE—ENM— ◇CCC/MR
France	PAL
Germany (East)	MEK
Germany (West)	HK—NA—WEK
Japan	FNR—HM—KRR—Mitsubishi—OSR—SEI—SR
Peru	C de P—C P Peru
Poland	HML—HMG
Portugal	CUF
S. Africa	PMC
Spain	CEM—ECSA
Sweden	Boliden Koppar
United Kingdom	E★R—RCB
USA	ALS—ATR—BER—B & M—DRW Ⓝᴱᶜ
	LNS—PA—P★D—T
USSR	MI
Zaire	UMK
Zambia	MCM—NCR—REC

Higher grade: cathodes

Australia	Erands—ISA
Belgium	UMK
Canada	CCR—ORC
Chile	AE—CCC—ENM
Finland	OKM
France	PAL
Germany (West)	KER—NA-ES
Japan	Dowa—FNR—Mitsubishi—Mitsui—OSR—SR— Sumiko 'N'—Sumiko 'T'—Tamano
Korea (South)	Onsan
Peru	MP-ILO
Poland	HMG-s
S. Africa	PMC
Spain	RTM
Sweden	Boliden —Boliden Koppar
USA	KE—KUE
Yugoslavia	BOR
Zambia	MCM—Mufulira—NCR—REC

Standard cathodes

Electrolytic copper in the form of cathodes assaying not less than 99.90% of copper (*silver being counted as copper*).

Austria	Brixlegg
Belgium	ME
Bulgaria	MK
China	Mimet
Germany (East)	MEK
Germany (West)	CF—DK—HL—NA—WEK
Hungary	CSMW
Italy	ATC—Rifometal—SMI
Japan	Dowa Okayama—HM—Mitsubishi 0 —Sumiko
Korea (South)	KMS
Mexico	CDM
Norway	FEC
Peru	C de P
	———
	Peru
	C P Peru
Poland	HMG—HML
Portugal	CUF
Spain	CEM—ECSA—Indumetal—MYC—SIA
United Kingdom	Actid—AM & S—ELK—Enthoven—JB—Melton Cathode Copper—MKB—RCB (max. size 44 in. × 44 in.)

USA	ATR—B & M—BER—CDS—CME—DRW— LMC—Magna—PA—RMR—T
USSR	MO—MOK
Zimbabwe	Inyati—Mangula

Fire refined

Class A

High grade fire refined copper assaying not less than 99.88% of copper (*silver being counted as copper*) in the form of ingots or ingotbars.

★ ★ ★

Chile	MB—MR
Germany (West)	BKR2—NA
S. Africa	MTD
United Kingdom	EFF—JB—MC3—MX—PRE
USA	Q—R
Zimbabwe	MRSR

Class B

Fire refined copper assaying not less than 99.70% of copper (*silver being counted as copper*) in the form of ingots or ingotbars.

Belgium	MF
Germany (West)	BKR1
United Kingdom	BE BS DE—E—GMU—JBBS Mersey—PRE75—Yellow Spot MXY—WBMR

TIN BRANDS

Official list issued by the Committee of the London Metal Exchange of brands of Tin deliverable in fulfilment of contracts for Standard Tin and High Grade Tin. High Grade Tin brands are deliverable against the Standard Tin contract.

Tin deliverable against the Standard Contract and the High Grade Contract shall be in ingots or slabs not less than about 12 kg nor more than about 50 kg.

Standard tin

Australia	Pyrmont OT Lempriere & Co.
Denmark	Bera Refined Tin (Lion with Ox-head)
France	Long Standard
Germany (East)	F
Germany (West)	M Standard NA Zinnwerke Wilhelmsburg

Malaysia	OTS
Netherlands	Tulip
	Windmill Star
Portugal	Embel
Rwanda	Somirwa
Singapore	Kimetal
Spain	Concha
	Mesae
	Reina Isabel B
United Kingdom	Associated Lead
	Chempur
	Cornish
	Hawthorne
	Melton Standard
	Penpoll
	River
	W H & Co. Mellanear
Zaire	Geomines

High grade tin

Australia	ATS
	ATS Low Arsenic Refined Tin
Belgium	UMHK
Bolivia	ENAF
Brazil	Bera Brasil
	Best
	Brasil-Monsa
	Cesbra
	Mamore
	Trevo
Germany (West)	M Spezial
	Rose
	Tree
Indonesia	Banka
	Mentok
Malaysia	ES Coy Ltd Straits Refined Tin
	Malaysia Smelting Corporation
	Straits Trading Company Limited
Netherlands	Billiton
	Windmill I
	Windmill II
	Windmill III
Nigeria	Makeri
Singapore	Watten Metals

S. Africa	Rooiberg
Spain	Concha A
	Mesae 99.9
Thailand	Lotus
	Thaisarco
United Kingdom	British HG
	Pass No. 1
	Pass USA Grade A
USA	Double Circle
	GCMC
	MRI
USSR	XXX
Zimbabwe	Jupiter

LEAD BRANDS

Official list issued by the Committee of the London Metal Exchange of brands of Refined Pig Lead deliverable in fulfilment of contracts for Standard Lead.

Refined Pig Lead deliverable against the Standard Contract shall be in pigs weighing not more than 50 kg each.

Australia	BHAS Lead 99.97

Belgium	Campine ER
	Hoboken Extra Raffine
	MCR Made in Belgium
	Veille Montagne ★ ★ ★
	99.97% + Fabrique Belgique 99.97% +
Bulgaria	KU₁ M
	O U₁ 3
Burma	BM Refined
Canada	BM & S
	Canada Metal
	MBC
	Tadanac
	Tonolli Canada
	TRS
Denmark	Bera
Eire	DMC
	MRL
Finland	Vermont

183

France	Penarroya
	SMMP
Germany (East)	F
Germany (West)	BHAS—West Germany—99.985%
	Braubach Dopp Raff B (Deutschland)
	BSB
	EschweilerRaffine
	Harz W 99.97
	NA (Norddeutsche Affinerie) E 99.99
	NA (Norddeutsche Affinerie) F 99.985
	NA (Norddeutsche Affinerie) H 99.97
	Raffiniertes Harz Blei
	Stolberg
Italy	AT & C
	Italpiombo
	MAK—1
	Monteponi
	Pertusola
Japan	Dowa
	ESS
	TAK
	EMK—K
	EMK—T
	SK
	Three Diamond
Korea (North)	KM
Mexico	Asarco
	CMFyAM Mexico
	IMM-Chihuahua
	MP-MP
	Penoles
Morocco	PZ Maroc
Namibia	TCL
	Tsumco
Netherlands	Saturnas
	Tulp
Peru	Cerro-Peru
	C de P Peru Industria Peruana
	C P Peru Industria Peruana
Poland	H2OMS
Spain	Cia La Cruz-Linares-Espana
	Guindos Doble Refinado
	Penarroya Importe d'Espagne
	RCA

Sweden	Bera
	Boliden A
	Boliden B
Tunisia	Penarroya Tunisie
	SMMT
United Kingdom	Afco
	Associated Lead
	BL Co.
	BLCO 99.97%
	BLCO 99.99%
	BLM
	BRU
	DX
	Emo
	GMU
	H J Enthoven & Sons Ltd.
	HM Lead 99.97%
	Holyrood
	LAA
	Melton Refined Lead
	PM
	Thames 99.99+
USA	Bunker Hill
	Doe Run
	GBC
	Glover
	Gould
	M
	Master Metals
	NL Ind
	Omaha and Grant
	Rainbow
	Revere
	RMC
	Sanders
	Schuylkill
	Seitzingers
	Southern Star
	Southwest
	Tonolli America
	USS Electro (non-electrolytically produced)
USSR	Ykcuk
Yugoslavia	Trepca
Zambia	Sable 99.99 +
	ZBHD

ZINC BRANDS

Official list issued by the Committee of the London Metal Exchange of brands of Zinc deliverable in fulfilment of contracts for Standard Zinc.

Zinc deliverable against the Standard Contract shall be in slabs, plates or ingots weighing not more than 55 kg each.

Algeria	SNS 99.9% +
	SNS 99.995% +
Australia	AZ
	AZ PW
	BHAS 99.95 +
	BHAS 99.99 +
	BHAS PW
	Derwent Prime
Austria	BBU 99.99
Belgium	Overcor 99.995
	Prayon
	Rothem
	UO Raffine
	★★★ VM Fabrique en Belgique
Bulgaria	H Р Б / K U₁ M
	H Р Б / O U₁ 3
Canada	Hudson Bay High-Grade Zinc
	Hudson Bay (Prime Western) Zinc
	Hudson Bay Special High-Grade Zinc
	Tadanac (Prime Western)
Finland	Outokumpo
France	Penarroya Z6
	RCA Special
	SMMP
Germany (East)	F
Germany (West)	★★★ Alternberg
	DKH
	Fah. Harz Zink 98.5
	Harz Zink 99.5
	Huettenzink Harz 99.5
	MHD
	RMZ
	SS
	Weser Extra Raff
	Wesser Zink 98.5

Italy	Elett MP
	Monteponi
	Pertusola 99.97%
	Pertusola 99.99%
	Portovesme
	Portovesme 99.995
Japan	M M C
	H
	M M C
	M
	MSC
	MSC RI
	SK
	SK SHG
	Three Diamond
	Toho
Korea (North)	KM
Korea (South)	KZ-HG
	KZ-SHG
	YP-HG
	YP-SHG
Mexico	Contimex
	IMM-Rosita
	Penoles
	Rosita
	Zincamex
Netherlands	Campine
Norway	Norzink Elektro
	Norzink Elektro 99.99 +
Peru	Cerro-Peru
	C de P Industria Peruana Peru 99.99 +
	C de P Industria Peruana Peru (Prime Western)
	CP Industria Peruana 99.99
Poland	EO
	Polsk Raf
Rumania	Zn D 1
S. Africa	Zincor ZNI
	Sinkor
Spain	Astuzinc Electro 99.95
	Astuzinc Electro 99.99 +
	EDZ
	MQN

United Kingdom	AM & S Zn4
	Avonmouth
	Imperial Avonmouth Smelting
	Imperial Severn Smelting
	Imperial Swansea Vale Smelting
	MS
	Severn
	Swansea Vale
USA	Amarillo
	Amax
	Amco (Prime Western)
	Amco-Blackwell
	Asarco Electro
	Bunker Hill
	Granby D
	HNP
	Lehigh
	M & H
	Meadow Brook
	National
	NZ / ZN
	P 1
	PSN
	St Joe
USSR	Ykcuk
	UB
Yugoslavia	Celje
	Zletovo
	Zorka
Zaire	UZK
Zambia	Sable 98.5 +

SILVER BRANDS

Official List issued by the Committee of the London Metal Exchange of brands of Silver deliverable in fulfilment of contracts for Silver.

Silver deliverable against the Fine Silver Contract shall be in the form of bars in the weight range 450 to 1250 troy ounces.

Argentina	Stella
Australia	BHAS
	ESA
	Erands

Belgium	Société Générale Métallurgique de Hoboken SA
	Hoboken 999.7 +
	Hoboken 999 +
Bulgaria	M
Burma	Burma Mines
Canada	CCR
	ORC
	Tadanac
France	Comptoir Lyon
	MBLG
	Compagnie des Métaux Précieux
Germany (East)	Mansfeld
Germany (West)	Degussa
	Heraeus
	Norddeutsche Affinerie
Italy	MP
	Vieri
	Vimet
Japan	Dowa
	HM
	NSS
	Three Diamond
	Yokohama Kinzoku
Mexico	Asarco-Monterrey
	Cia Minera de Penoles SA
	Cia Metalurgica Penoles SA
	IMM-Monterrey
	Metalurgica Mexicana Penoles SA
	R del M
	SAM
Namibia	TCL
Netherlands	Smelting Schones
	HDZ
Peru	C de P
	C P Peru
Poland	ZTM
S. Africa	RRLd
Spain	Orispania
	Penarroya
	Socemp
Sweden	Boliden Silver (999)
Switzerland	MP Métaux Précieux SA

189

United Kingdom	BL Co
	Engelhard London
	JM
	JMC
	JMCF
	Johnson Matthey London 999
	JSCF
	JSW
	R
	SS Co
USA	Asarco Amarillo Texas
	Asarco-Baltimore
	Asarco-Perth Amboy
	Asarco-Selby
	AS & R Co-Baltimore
	AS & R Co-Perth Amboy
	San Francisco, Cal.
	Selby Gold & Silver Refinery
	Balbach
	BER
	Bunker Hill
	DRW
	E
	IMS
	ISR
	KUE
	Raritan
	Seal of the USA
	S-M *(Warrants issued on and after October 1978 not good delivery)*
	UMS Co.
	USS Co.
USSR	CCCP
Yugoslavia	BOR
	Trepca
Zambia	NCR

ALUMINIUM BRANDS

The production of the following listed producers shall constitute good delivery under the Aluminium Contract, provided that such production conforms to the terms and conditions of the Contract.

190

Country	Company	Brand
EUROPE		
Austria	Salzburger Aluminium GmbH	SAG
	Vereinigte Metallwerke	ALU
	Ranshofen-Bendorf AG	Ranshofen
Czechoslavakia	ZSNP Kovohute Praha	
France	Aluminium Pechiney	Pechiney
Germany (East)	Lauta Werke	Mansfeld
	VEB Elektrochemische Kombinat	
Germany (West)	Aluminium-Hütte Rheinfelden GmbH	Rheinfelden
	Vereinigte Aluminium-Werke AG	VAW
	Kaiser Aluminium Europe Inc.	KAPAL
	Leichmetall GmbH	LMG
	Gebrueder Giulini GmbH	
	Hamburger Aluminiumwerk GmbH	HAW
Greece	Aluminium de Grece	ADG
Hungary	Hungarian Aluminium Corporation	INOTA HUNGALU
Iceland	Icelandic Aluminium Co. Ltd.	ISAL
Italy	Alluminio Italia Spa	A Alluminio Italia AP-INA
	Alumetal	Alumetal
	Alsar SpA	Alsar
	Soc. Alluminio Veneto per Azioni (Sava)	SAVA
Netherlands	Aluminium Delfzijl BV	Delfzijl
	Pechiney Nederland NV	PNL
Norway	A/S Ardal og Sunndal Verk	ASV
	Norsk Hydro A/S Alnor	Alnor
	DNN Aluminium A/S	DNN
	Mosal Aluminium, Elkem-Spigerverket A/S & Co.	Mosal
	Sor Norge Aluminium A/S	Soral
Poland	Huta Aluminium	WR36 H 29
Rumania	Aluminium Enterprise Slatina	UAS
Spain	Empresa Nacional del Aluminio SA	Endasa Alcan
	Aluminio de Galicia SA	Alugasa

Country	Company	Brand
	Aluminio Espanol SA	Aluminio Espanol
Sweden	Graenges Aluminium AB	Graenges Aluminium
Switzerland	Aluminium Suisse SA	Alusuisse
	Usine d'Aluminium de Martigny	
Turkey	Etibank	
United Kingdom	The British Aluminium Co. Ltd (BACO)	BACO
	Alcan (UK) Ltd	ALCAN
	Anglesey Aluminium Metal Ltd	AAM
USSR	Raznoimport	CCCP
	Ministry of Foreign Trade of	HKA 3
	the USSR, Smolenskaya—	ID
	Sonnaya Pl., 32–34 Moscow	KPA 3
	121200, USSR	NPKA 3
Yugoslavia	Tvornica Lakih Metala (TLM) (Boris Kidric)	.TLM (Boris Kidric)
	Tovarna Glinice in Aluminija (Boris Kidric)	TGA
	Kombinat Aluminijuma Titograd (KAT)	KAT

AFRICA

Cameroon	Alucam	Alucam
Egypt	The Aluminium Company of Egypt	EGYPT
Ghana	Volta Aluminium Co. (Valco)	Valco
S. Africa	Alusaf (Pty) Ltd	ALUSAF

AMERICA

Argentina	Aluminios Argentinos SA	ALUAR
Brazil	Alcan Aluminio do Brasil SA	Alcan Brasil
	Companhia Brasileira de Aluminio SA	
	Companhia Mineira de Aluminio	
	Aluminio do Brasil Nordeste SA	
Canada	Alcan (Aluminium Company of Canada Ltd)	Alcan
	Canadian Reynolds Metals Co. Ltd	

Country	Company	Brand
Mexico	Aluminio SA de CV	Alumsa
Surinam	Suriname Aluminium Co.	SURALCO
USA	Alcoa (Aluminium Company of America)	Alcoa
	Anaconda Aluminium Co.	
	Martin Marietta Aluminium Inc.	Martin Marietta
	Reynolds Metal Co.	Reynolds
	Kaiser Aluminium & Chemical Corp.	Kaiser
	Consolidated Aluminium Corp.	Conalco
	Intalco Aluminium Corp.	CASTMAX
	Eastalco Aluminium Co.	
	Ormet Corp.	
	Revere Copper and Brass Inc.	R
	National Southwire Aluminium Co. (NSA)	
	Noranda Aluminium Inc.	
Venezuela	Aluminio del Caronie SA	ALCASA
	New Venalum SA	VENALUM
ASIA		
Bahrain	Aluminium Bahrain Co.	ALBA
China	China National Metals & Minerals, Import and Export Corporation, Erh Li Kou, Peking.	
India	Aluminium Corp. of India Ltd	JK-ACI
	Hindustan Aluminium Corp.	HINDALCO
	Indian Aluminium Co. Ltd	Word Indal
	Madras Aluminium Co. Ltd	
	Bharat Aluminium Co. Ltd	BALCO
Iran	Iran Aluminium Co.	Iralco
Japan	Showa Aluminium Industries KK	SDK
	Nippon Light Metal Co. Ltd	KK
	Sumitomo Aluminium Smelting Co.	
	Mitsubishi Light Metal Industries	MCI
	Mitsui Aluminium Co. Ltd	ALM
	Sumikei Aluminium Industries Ltd	

Country	Company	Brand
Korea (South)	Aluminium of Korea Ltd	Koralu
Taiwan	Taiwan Aluminium Corp.	TALCO
United Arab Emirates	Dubai Aluminium Co. Ltd	DUBAL

OCEANIA

Australia	Comalco Aluminium (Bell Bay) Ltd	Comalco
	Alcoa of Australia Ltd	
	Alcan Australia Ltd	Alcan
New Zealand	New Zealand Aluminium Smelters Ltd	NZAS

NICKEL PRODUCERS

The production of the following listed producers shall constitute good delivery under the Primary Nickel Contract, provided that such production conforms to the terms and conditions of the Contract.

Production from	Location
Selcast Exploration Ltd, 50 St George's Terrace, Perth, Western Australia 6000	Spargoville Mine, Western Australia
Western Mining Corp. Ltd, 459 Collins Street, Melbourne 3000, Australia	Kwinana, Australia
INCO Ltd, 1 First Canadian Place, Toronto, Ontario, Canada	Sudbury, Canada; Thompson, Canada; Clydach, UK
Sherritt Gordon Mines Ltd, 2800 Commerce Court West, Toronto, Ontario, Canada	Ford Saskatchewan, Alberta, Canada
Outokumpu Oy, Toolonkatu 4, SF 00101, Helsinki, Finland	Harjavalta, Finland

Production from	Location
Société Metallurgique Le Nickel—SLN, Tour Maine Montparnasse, 33 Avenue du Maine, 75751 Paris Cedex 15, France	Le Havre, France
Sumitomo Metal Mining Co. Ltd, 11-3, 5-Chome, Shimbashi, Minato-Ku, Tokyo, Japan	Niihama, Japan
Shimura Kako Co. Ltd, 2-18-1 Higashi—Sakashita, Habashiku—Tokyo, Japan	Shimura, Japan
Falconbridge Nickel Mines Ltd, Commerce Court West, Toronto, Ontario, Canada	Kristiansand, Norway
Marinduque Mining & Industrial Corp., 2283 Pasong Tamo Ext., Makati, Rizal, Philippines	Nonoc Island, Philippines
Impala Platinum Ltd, Unicorn House, 70 Marshall Street, Johannesburg 2001, South Africa	Springs, South Africa
Rustenburg Platinum Holdings Ltd, Consolidated Bldgs, Fox and Harrison Streets, Johannesburg 2001	Brand: Matthey Nickel (as produced after 1/4/80); Rustenburg, South Africa
Amax Inc., Amax Center, Greenwich, Connecticut 06830, USA	Port Nickel, USA Braithwaite, USA
Raznoimport, Moscow	Norilsk, USSR
Rio Tinto Mining (Zimbabwe) Ltd, 61 Samora Machel Ave., Harare, Zimbabwe	Eiffel Flats, Zimbabwe

Appendix 4

Example of an LME Contract

© London Metal Exchange   **Authorised 27th May, 1980**

STANDARD TIN CONTRACT FORM

Approved by the Board of Directors and by the Committee of the LONDON METAL EXCHANGE

Contract B

LONDON ....

M...

$\frac{I}{We}$ have this day $\frac{\text{sold to}}{\text{bought from}}$ .you, according and subject to the Rules and Regulations of the London Metal Exchange,

....

....Tons (two per cent. either more

or less and subject to Rule 3 below) of

STANDARD TIN

Price £ .... per ton of 1000 kilogrammes

net $\dfrac{\text{plus}}{\text{minus}}$ % to us

....

The appropriate Import Duty (if any) ruling on the prompt date to be for Buyer's Account.

Prompt ....

We have the right at any time on demand to require you to pay us such a sum (hereinafter referred to as a "margin") in cash and/or to deposit with us security in such other form and of such amount not exceeding the value of the contract as we in our discretion require and in order to secure the due fulfilment by you of your obligations under this contract and to the intent that the value of the margin in relation to the contract shall at all times during the currency of the contract be maintained by you we have the further right on demand and whether in one or more calls to require you to pay to us the difference between the value of the contract at the time of entering into the same and the current market value at any time thereafter as we in our discretion require. In the event of any failure by you to fulfil your obligations we have an immediate right of appropriation of any such cash and/or to sell any security to satisfy our rights as above in addition to all other rights reserved to us by this contract.

This contract is made between ourselves and yourselves as principals, we alone being liable to you for its performance. The percentage (if any) charged by us to you is to be regarded simply as part of the price and may be shared by us with agents introducing the business, whilst we reserve the right also to charge a percentage or commission to any person from or to whom we may have bought or sold to cover our liability hereunder.

In the event of your failing to meet your engagements arising out of this or any other outstanding contract or contracts between us which are subject to the Rules and Regulations of the London Metal Exchange whether by failing to provide on the due date documents to meet sales or money to take up documents (as the case may be) or otherwise howsoever or of your failing to supply or maintain such margin (if any) for which we are entitled to call and have called or in the event of your suspending payment or becoming bankrupt or committing any act of bankruptcy or (being a Company) in the event of your going into liquidation whether voluntary or otherwise, we reserve the right to close this contract and any other said outstanding contract or contracts if as and when we in our sole discretion shall so decide by selling out or buying in against you (as the case may be) and any differences arising therefrom shall be payable forthwith notwithstanding that the prompt day or other day originally stipulated for settlement may not have arrived.

Any delay in our enforcing any of our rights under this contract shall not be deemed to constitute a waiver thereof.

Members of the London Metal Exchange

SPECIAL RULES FOR STANDARD TIN

1. Quality. The tin delivered under this contract must be refined tin assaying not less than 99·75 per cent. Sn.

All tin delivered must be:

(i) of brands listed in the LME approved list of Standard Tin brands;

(ii) either in ingots or slabs each weighing not less than 12 kgs or more than about 50 kgs.

2. Settlement. Contracts shall be settled on exact quantities of 5 tons at the official settlement price quoted by the Committee operative on the prompt date, buyer and seller paying or receiving, as the case may be, the difference, if any, between the settlement price and the contract price.

3. Delivery. The tin shall be delivered on the prompt date in any warehouse listed for this purpose with the Committee at listed delivery points in seller's option. (Names of such warehouses can be obtained from the London Metal Exchange Office). Warrants tendered in fulfilment of contracts shall be invoiced at the settlement price mentioned in Rule 2 above in parcels each of 5 tons or a multiple thereof (each 5 tons to be treated as a separate contract). The tin shall have been weighed in drafts of either 500 kilogrammes or 1 ton each and the warrants shall be for 5 tons each (two per cent either more or less). Warrants issued prior to the 1st January, 1970 for long tons shall constitute good delivery provided that their weights are within a 2% tolerance of 5 long tons. Each parcel of 5 tons shall be of one brand, shape and size subject to the necessity of including different shapes and sizes at the bottom of each parcel for the purpose of palletisation, and shall lie at one warehouse. Rent shall be allowed on the invoice.

4. Weights. The word "ton" wherever appearing in the contract shall be a metric tonne of 1000 kilogrammes. In the case of warrants where weights are shown in long tons conversion shall be at the rate of 1 long ton to 1016 kilogrammes. Warrant weights in all cases shall be accepted as between buyer and seller.

5. Warrants. Each warrant must state the brand and the number of ingots or slabs comprising each parcel.

6. Disputes. Any question concerning formation and any dispute under this contract shall be notified to the Secretary of the London Metal Exchange in writing by the seller or the buyer or both of them jointly. Such question or dispute if not settled by agreement shall be referred to arbitration in accordance with the Rules and Regulations of the London Metal Exchange. The decision in writing of the Appeal Committee from the Award of the Arbitrators shall be a condition precedent to a Notice of Motion to remit or set aside the Award of the Arbitrators and the decision of the Appeal Committee or to an action being brought.

Neither the Board nor Committee, nor the Monitoring Committee of the Metal Market & Exchange Co. Limited nor any member of any of them nor any Trustee appointed by the Directors shall be under any liability whatsoever either in contract or in tort in respect of any decision, statement, act or omission whether negligent or otherwise taken made performed or omitted in connection with the monitoring operation carried on by and on behalf of the Metal Market & Exchange Co. Limited.

The Uniform Law concerning the formation of contracts for the International Sale of Goods and the Uniform Law regulating the International Sale of Goods shall not apply.

(In the above Rules "The Committee" means the Committee of the London Metal Exchange)

199

Index